# Access Audit Handbook

Alison Grant
Centre for Accessible Environments

RIBA Publishing

FSC
www.fsc.org
MIX
Paper from
responsible sources
FSC® C016201

© Centre for Accessible Environments and RIBA Publishing, 2013

Published by RIBA Publishing, 15 Bonhill Street, London EC2P 2EA

ISBN 978 1 85946 492 2

Stock code 79860

Original front and back cover illustrations drawn by Alison Grant.

British Library Cataloguing in Publications Data
A catalogue record for this book is available from the British Library.

CAE Publications Project Manager and Editor: Geraldine McNamara
Commissioning Editors: Lucy Harbor and Steven Cross
Project Editor: Neil O'Regan
Designed and typeset by: Steve Paveley Design
Printed and bound by: W.G. Baird, Antrim

RIBA Publishing is part of RIBA Enterprises Ltd.
www.ribaenterprises.com

# Contents

## Acknowledgments

We wish to acknowledge the help provided by the following organisations
in the preparation of this publication:

Almeida Theatre
Arts Access Australia
Changing Places Consortium
Eden Project
Eurotunnel
Hebden Bridge Town Hall
St John's Notting Hill
ZSL London Zoo

Photographs of Hebden Bridge Town Hall supplied courtesy of Jade Smith

# 1.0 Introduction

## Who should use this handbook?

This handbook is aimed at experienced access professionals, as well as people who are new to access auditing, who may include:

- business owners, managers and other service providers
- architects
- surveyors
- interior designers
- building and facilities managers
- access groups

- access officers
- building control officers
- equality and diversity officers
- customer services managers
- human resources staff
- health and safety officers
- occupational therapists

The handbook explains what an access audit is and its purpose within the process of identifying, planning and implementing improvements to make buildings, environments and services more inclusive.

Undertaking an access audit is considered good practice and is an effective way of exploring potential barriers to access. The handbook also sets out the legislative context for undertaking access audits in acknowledgement that many audits are commissioned in response to duties under equality legislation. The handbook provides detailed guidance on how to undertake an audit survey and explains what an audit should include and how to go about it in practice. Communicating the results of an access audit effectively is critically important so that clients are able to understand and consider recommendations in the context of their business or organisation. The section covering report writing describes the different ways of recording the findings of an audit and setting out recommendations for implementing change. For clients who are commissioning an access audit, the handbook includes useful information on issues that should be considered before appointing an access auditor or consultant. The importance of user participation and consultation is also set out in recognition of the valuable contribution that staff, volunteers, regular visitors, access groups and relevant professionals can make to the access audit process.

Access auditing is a complex activity and people new to the field are encouraged to undergo training. It can also be beneficial to gain experience of access auditing by working alongside an experienced access professional.

This handbook is intended to be used together with the CAE / RIBA Publishing guide *Designing for Accessibility* (2012 edition). The checklists in this handbook, which provide a useful starting point when commencing an audit, correlate closely with the technical guidance in *Designing for Accessibility*.

# 2.0 Access audits

## 2.1 What is an access audit?

An access audit is a means of assessing features of an environment (building or external area) and services in terms of accessibility. Although now well established, access audits remain an evolving concept and may mean different things to different people. An access audit is a measure of how well the environment and method of service delivery meet the needs of existing and potential users, whether they be staff, visitors, volunteers, pupils, patients, students or others. It is also a process through which potential barriers to access may be identified and recorded alongside suggested improvements in a way that enables people responsible for a site, building or service to move on to the next step of planning and implementing change.

Access audits have evolved over time – they have been undertaken by specialist consultants, architects, occupational therapists and disabled people for many years as a means of assessing an existing environment and services, and identifying potential improvements to facilitate access.

An assessment of access provision in either existing buildings or proposed developments has been a core requirement of some funding bodies for many years, notably the City Bridge Trust (in London), Arts Council of England and other National Lottery distributors.

The increase in prevalence of access audits over the last decade was undoubtedly prompted by the duties placed on employers and service providers under the Disability Discrimination Acts 1995 and 2005. Under these Acts, employers and service providers were required to make reasonable adjustments to policies, practices, procedures and premises where any of these created a potential barrier to disabled people. The role of an access audit became firmly established as a means of identifying reasonable adjustments and a starting point in the process of implementing change. In England, Scotland and Wales, the Equality Act 2010 has replaced the Disability Discrimination Acts and other single-issue legislation with a single Act, but continues to identify access audits as a key measure of identifying reasonable adjustments – this is discussed in more detail below.

Carrying out an access audit comprises a series of tasks, typically starting with briefing / data gathering, followed by a detailed site survey, consultation with building users and the preparation of a written report to record and communicate the outcome of the audit. Guidelines for commissioned audits are set out at the end of this chapter under the heading *Commissioning an access audit*. The more practical elements of the audit, such as the site survey and consultation with building users, are discussed in chapter 3 *Audit methodology* and guidelines for recording the audit data and recommendations in chapter 4 *Report writing*.

The basic principle of an access audit is comprehensively to assess the accessibility of an environment, its facilities and any services delivered from it. To do this, the auditor must take into account all existing and prospective building users and consider any potential barriers that may render part of a building or a service inaccessible or difficult to use by any particular group of users. Depending on the environment, facility or service being audited, consideration should be given to people who are service users, employees, volunteers and students or pupils in an education environment.

The Centre for Accessible Environments defines an access audit as a means of:

- examining the accessibility of services and facilities
- identifying where physical barriers may compromise access to services by assessing the feature against predetermined criteria
- measuring the 'usability' of facilities within a building and the services being delivered in it

## 2.2 Access audits and the Equality Act 2010

The Equality Act 2010 (the Act) replaced existing anti-discrimination legislation with a single Act and applies in England, Scotland and Wales. The Act unified legislation that previously covered different aspects of discrimination separately. Most of the Act came into force in October 2010; other aspects, including the public sector Equality Duty, came into force in April 2011. Previous legislation, including the Disability Discrimination Acts 1995 and 2005, are now repealed. (In Northern Ireland, the Disability Discrimination Acts 1995 and 2005 and other single-issue equality legislation still apply.)

The Act protects people from discrimination on a range of grounds, which it refers to as 'protected characteristics'. These are:
- age
- disability
- gender reassignment
- marriage and civil partnership
- pregnancy and maternity
- race
- religion or belief
- sex and sexual orientation

A cornerstone of the Act is the duty to make reasonable adjustments to ensure that disabled people are not substantially disadvantaged when compared with non-disabled people. The duty to make reasonable adjustments relates only to disabled people – it does not relate to people on the basis of any of the other protected characteristics.

The link between access audits and the duty to make reasonable adjustments was clearly established in the Codes of Practice to the Disability Discrimination Act 1995. These specifically referred to an access audit as a means of identifying improvements from which an access plan or strategy could be developed.

The Code of Practice to Part 3 (services and public functions) and Part 7 (associations) of the Equality Act 2010 also identifies access audits as a means by which service providers are able to identify reasonable adjustments. The Code of Practice states:

3.42 In relation to the duty to make reasonable adjustments for disabled people, the following actions will help service providers to meet their obligations under the Act:
- Review regularly whether services are accessible to disabled people
- Carry out and act on the results of an access audit carried out by a suitably qualified person
- Provide regular training to staff which is relevant to the adjustments to be made
- Review regularly the effectiveness of reasonable adjustments and act on the findings of those reviews

**Reasonable adjustments in Practice**

7.80 When a service provider is considering making reasonable adjustments, the following measures may be helpful and constitute good practice that may help avoid acts of discrimination. In some circumstances, they may either be a means to identify reasonable adjustments or actually constitute reasonable adjustments themselves:

- planning in advance for the requirements of disabled people and reviewing the reasonable adjustments in place
- conducting access audits on premises
- asking disabled customers for their views on reasonable adjustments
- consulting local and national disability groups
- drawing disabled people's attention to relevant reasonable adjustments so they know they can use the service
- properly maintaining auxiliary aids and having contingency plans in place in case of the failure of the auxiliary aid
- training employees to appreciate how to respond to requests for reasonable adjustments
- encouraging employees to develop additional serving skills for disabled people (for example, communicating with hearing impaired people); and
- ensuring that employees are aware of the duty to make reasonable adjustments and understand how to communicate with disabled customers so that reasonable adjustments can be identified and made

Equality Act 2010 Code of Practice
Services, public functions and associations

Access audits are not only relevant to service providers. Employers have a duty under Part 5 of the Act to make reasonable adjustments to ensure that disabled people can access and progress in employment. The duty to make reasonable adjustments applies to all employers, whether they are small or large organisations, although what is considered reasonable for different employers to undertake will vary according to the employer's circumstances.

Under Part 6 of the Act, further and higher education providers have a duty to make reasonable adjustments to ensure that disabled students are able to access and participate in all aspects of learning and to enjoy the other benefits, facilities and services associated with their education. In schools, the Act introduces a duty to make reasonable adjustments in relation to the provision of auxiliary aids and services. The duty to make reasonable adjustments to physical features of school premises is already covered by the accessibility planning duties.

The public sector Equality Duty, which has been implemented to ensure that public bodies play their part in making society fairer, came into force in April 2011 and replaced the previous separate disability, gender and race equality duties. The aims of the duty are three-fold:
• to eliminate unlawful discrimination, victimisation and harassment
• to promote equality of opportunity for all
• to foster good relations, promote understanding and challenge prejudice

Underpinning the Equality Duty is the expectation that public bodies actively engage with people with different protected characteristics as a means of identifying appropriate solutions to potential barriers, to prioritise aims and help in the development of effective policies. Engagement sits comfortably alongside the access audit process and provides an invaluable contribution to ongoing decision-making and the formulation of an access plan or strategy for implementing change.

## 2.3 Access audits, access strategy and the planning and building regulations process

The preparation and submission of an access strategy has been required for some years now to accompany applications for planning and listed building consent and for approval under the building regulations. (Some applications relating to existing dwellings are exempt from this requirement, as are planning applications that relate to works other than buildings.)

At the planning application stage, the access strategy is often incorporated into the broader document referred to as a design and access strategy. The design and access strategy describes how a design has evolved and how provisions for access have been incorporated.

In many cases, such as where a proposed development includes changes to an existing environment, the access strategy naturally evolves from an access audit and explains how existing barriers are to be overcome or improved.

Under the building regulations, an access strategy is required to accompany applications for non-domestic buildings and should describe how access has been incorporated into the design. An access strategy submitted at this stage should be a development of the access strategy submitted at the planning stage – it is not a separate document, but an evolution of the same document which is updated as the design progresses. Where features of the proposed building work deviate from guidance in Approved Document M: Access to and use of buildings (2004 edition incorporating 2010 and 2013 amendments) the access strategy should explain why this is the case and how the adopted design satisfies the regulations.

At both the planning and building regulations stages, the access strategy should record the outcomes of consultation exercises with disabled people, local interest groups and specialist advisors.

The National Planning Policy Framework, which was published in March 2012, sets out the government's reforms to the planning system in England, which are focused on simplifying the planning system, making it more accessible, protecting the environment and promoting sustainable growth. Key to the Framework is engagement with local communities and the development of neighbourhoods and communities. Engagement at all stages of the planning and design process is essential to meet local need and to ensure environments are inclusive.

## 2.4 What follows an access audit?

An access audit is the first stage in the process of identifying, planning and implementing change. An access audit should not be considered as achieving an end in itself, but rather a means by which people responsible for a physical environment or service can move forward towards the preparation of an access plan or strategy and the effective implementation of adjustments, whether they be operational, management or physical changes.

The Code of Practice to Part 3 and Part 7 acknowledges that conducting an access audit is part of a process and that acting on the outcomes of an audit is key to meeting obligations under the Act. Importantly, the Code highlights that conducting an access audit and acting on the outcomes may mitigate the likelihood of claims of alleged discrimination.

There may be instances where subsequent audits are undertaken of the same premises or service, for example as a part of a continual cycle of review. An access audit is, by nature, a record of a building and its functions at one particular moment in time – it records the features and arrangements in place when the audit was undertaken. Following the audit, adjustments should be put in place which result in the removal of barriers and an improvement in the way services are delivered. Implementation of changes will clearly mark an improvement in accessibility, but should not be regarded as a fait accompli. The Code of Practice encourages service providers to regularly review the way in which services are provided, not simply to consider the issue as a one-off exercise. One way of achieving this is to undertake periodic audits or to review and update an audit previously undertaken. Undertaking a subsequent audit may be appropriate if the building has been refurbished or if the nature of the client or service provider's business has changed. Undertaking a subsequent audit may provide the best opportunity to update recommendations in line with developing legislation and best practice design guidance.

The case study in chapter 6 illustrates how a service provider has moved forwards from an initial access audit to plan and implement improvements to transform an inaccessible historic building into a thriving multi-use development.

## 2.5 Commissioning an access audit

Where an access audit is to be undertaken by a person (or persons) outside the client organisation, the fees, timescale, terms of engagement and scope of works should be clarified at an early stage and clearly set out to record the agreement between the client and auditor. The items in the inset box on page 12 provide a checklist for both clients and auditors.

**Commissioning an access audit – issues for the client and auditor to consider:**

**Terms and conditions of appointment** – For the benefit and protection of both client and auditor, the terms and conditions of appointment should be confirmed before the commencement of any commission. Terms and conditions should include the client's and auditor's duties under the agreement, payment mechanisms, levels of professional indemnity and other insurance cover, an understanding relating to confidentiality and copyright, any particular requirements relating to communication methods and a mechanism by which the agreement can be terminated and suspended. The Access Consultancy Services Schedule Supplement to the RIBA Forms of Appointment is a suitable model to use. The National Register of Access Consultants (NRAC) has produced a model *Terms and conditions for the engagement of an access consultant or auditor* and an *Engagement Agreement*, which are available to download from the NRAC website and can be used for the appointment of auditors and consultants who are or are not NRAC members.

**Professional fees** – Fees and any relevant expenses should be clearly established and agreed in writing before any work is undertaken by the auditor. Fees will relate to the project scope of works either provided by the client or agreed during discussions between the client and auditor.

**Scope of works / project brief** – The scope of works should establish which sites / buildings and which parts of a site, building or service are to be included in an audit. This may be particularly relevant where, for example, a client requires only the public facilities in a building to be audited and not the staff-only areas. The project brief should stipulate particular requirements in terms of the audit output, for example the type of report and any requirement for information such as priority ratings, categories and cost bands.

# 3.0 Audit methodology

## 3.1 The site survey

As with any survey, a planned and methodical approach is best. An audit survey, by its nature, is an assessment of the accessibility of an environment and its services, and so is best undertaken in a logical, sequential way. The audit survey follows the 'journey sequence' of arrival, entrance, circulation, facilities and exit. By replicating the sequence in which most people arrive at and use a building, the auditor can consider the suitability of the environment, its features and any potential physical or operational barriers. Importantly, the auditor should also consider how easy a building is to **exit** – this can easily be overlooked when the overall emphasis is on enabling people to get into and around buildings and facilitating easier access to services.

Larger and more complex buildings will have more than a single journey sequence. Some buildings may have multiple entrance and exit routes, separate areas providing distinct services and defined areas for public or staff-only access. The audit survey should be thorough and fully consider each area of the building, or each distinct area of service.

Depending on the nature of the client business or type of environment, an auditor may need to be accompanied during the audit survey. Where this is the case, it is useful to know in advance so that arrangements can be made and sufficient time allowed for undertaking the survey. Security clearance may also be required and this usually has to be arranged in advance of any visit.

It is preferable for a building to be audited when in use as this gives the best picture of how people actually access services and use the facilities. Auditing a building in use may also highlight where there is simply insufficient space for the number of people expected to use the facilities at any one time, a situation that could itself create a potential barrier to access. Auditing a building when it is empty or closed to the public may make the audit survey an easier task, but does not provide a true picture of how the building is actually used. If the main audit survey has, for practical or operational reasons, to be undertaken when the building is closed, a subsequent visit during normal operation is recommended.

Where rooms or areas of a site or building are inaccessible because they are locked, in use or because access has specifically been denied, these should be recorded in the audit survey. Clearly, where this is the case, the auditor is unable to assess or record any aspect of accessibility. To protect the auditor from future liabilities should there indeed be an issue with the area, a note should be made that the area was excluded from the survey and the reason for this.

If plans of the building are available, these can be a great help to the auditor, particularly if the building is large or complex. Studying the plans in advance of the audit survey can help the auditor to plan a route or strategy for the survey which will ensure that no areas are missed.

Having said this, where the site or building being audited is one that members of the public visit on a one-off or infrequent basis, it can be beneficial for the auditor to arrive 'cold', without any prior knowledge of where facilities are located or how the service operates. This will place the auditor in a similar position to a member of the public and provide first-hand experience of accessibility in terms of identifying the facility or service.

Where the auditor knows the site or building well it can be difficult to judge how members of the public, perhaps visiting for the first time, perceive the building and its services. Features can be easily overlooked, particularly in environments which are very familiar, and in such instances, potential barriers could be missed. It is essential in these circumstances for the auditor to consider the facilities from a fresh point of view and to bear in mind how first-time visitors or service users may perceive the environment.

## 3.2 What do you audit?

The elements covered in an access audit depend on the type and nature of the environment and services under consideration. Buildings and sites vary considerably and, although there will be common elements between particular types, no two access audits will be exactly the same. The way services are delivered may also differ between sites which are otherwise physically similar, due to varying policies, management procedures or staff attitude.

Any element covered in an access audit should be considered in the context of the particular environment, site, building or service. Characteristics of a building, for example whether or not the building is historically significant, are likely to affect the nature of recommendations in the audit, particularly where physical barriers are identified. Similarly, the nature of a service could affect a judgement made about a building feature. An example of this could be the lighting levels in a nightclub, which are typically very low and consequently do not meet current best practice guidelines. It would clearly not be appropriate to recommend a substantial change to the lighting levels as to do so would destroy the ambience of the nightclub.

There is no definitive list of physical features, aspects of services or management issues that must be covered by an audit, although the items in the inset table provide a guide to the categories which may be appropriate across a range of building and service types.

**Aspects of an environment and services to be considered in an audit:**

**Publicity and printed material** – Publicity material such as leaflets or pre-arrival maps and guides provide introductory information about a building or service and should be accessible to all potential visitors. Printed material may be the first point of contact a person has with a service provider, building or site and first-time visitors may make a decision on whether to visit a venue based on information contained in the document. Not all building occupiers or service providers will produce such information, but where they do and where it is an integral part of the overall information and wayfinding system, the accessibility of the information should be considered within the audit.

**Websites and online services** – Virtually all organisations are expected to have an online presence, particularly those providing services to the general public. As a minimum, organisations should provide contact details and an electronic means of contacting the organisation. For many organisations and companies, websites offer a service in their own right by providing a platform to access information, a vast array of services, products for purchase or download, and social media.

The way websites are designed and structured can significantly affect accessibility. Assessing the accessibility of a website is a specialist area and a detailed assessment of any online information is likely to be impractical for most auditors. However, auditors should familiarise themselves with best practice guidelines so that these can be highlighted to clients. Reference could be made in an audit report to current guidelines on web accessibility and highlight the key issues for web designers.

Organisations such as the Web Accessibility Initiative provide comprehensive guidance on making websites accessible to disabled people.

Web pages should be clear, logical, easy to navigate and compatible with a range of screen-reading software. This website demonstrates many aspects of good practice in relation to web accessibility as well as including an Auslan video translation on each main navigation page.

**Public transport links and approach routes** – Depending on the nature and location of the site, building or service provision, the availability of suitable public transport links may be relevant. The accessibility of the transport itself, the proximity of the nearest set-down point and the suitability of the route between the set-down point and the site are all relevant to the accessibility of a venue being audited. If an audit is being undertaken of a town or city centre, for example, the location of bus and tram stops and the railway station is particularly important, as are the pedestrian routes from these enroute to key facilities such as visitor attractions, shopping areas and local council offices.

Figure 3.1 This section of footpath is potentially hazardous to pedestrians and is likely to be difficult and uncomfortable for wheelchair users to traverse. Although it is not under the direct control of the nearby service provider who has commissioned an access audit, the condition of the approach route may affect the accessibility of the venue for some people. It can be useful to identify problematic features such as this so that service providers can recommend alternative approach routes in the shorter term at the same time as pursuing the local authority to undertake necessary repairs.

Figure 3.2 Although the litter on this approach route is not a permanent feature, it obstructs the footpath and could cause difficulties for pedestrians. The overhanging shrub also projects across the footpath and may cause problems for visually impaired people using a guide cane to detect the brick wall at the back of the footpath.

**Car parking and setting-down points** – The provision of suitable car parking close to the building or facility it serves is essential for disabled people, both as drivers and passengers of private vehicles. In venues such as visitor attractions, leisure and entertainment venues, the provision of larger spaces for adapted commercial vehicles and minibuses is also relevant, as is the provision of setting down and collection points for people using taxis or other vehicles. The overall provision, identification and size of parking bays should be audited, as well as detailed aspects such as suitability of the surfacing, the crossfall gradient and lighting.

Figure 3.3 These designated car parking bays have a number of good features such as their size, the hatched zones between and behind the bays for side and rear access and the post-mounted sign. The bays are also located on level ground, which is a good feature, but the surfacing (loose gravel within a plastic paving grid) is likely to present difficulties to people with mobility impairments and is also unsuitable for a ground-painted symbol. Gravel within a rigid plastic mesh needs to be well maintained and compacted to ensure it does not present difficulties to people with mobility impairments. Shrubs should be regularly trimmed to make sure they do not obscure signage.

**Pedestrian routes** – Path routes and external spaces provide essential access to and around buildings. They may provide a direct route from the edge of a site to the main entrance to a building, or link a series of buildings and facilities on a large campus. Some paths may also be designated emergency exit routes. An access audit should cover all aspects of the pedestrian route network, including suitability of the overall layout, gradients and changes in level, path widths, the provision of passing bays and rest areas, surfacing and drainage, lighting, wayfinding and hazard warning and protection.

Figure 3.4 The pedestrian routes in this environment provide access to a visitor attraction but also provide an amenity in themselves. The surface is well laid and firm, with gentle crossfall gradients and flush drainage covers positioned away from the main flow of pedestrians. The edge of the route is physically defined with seating and other street furniture and trees logically positioned to avoid causing an obstruction.

Figure 3.5 This sign provides interesting information about the park environment and is mounted at a suitable height, but is positioned away from the path where it is not easily accessible to wheelchair users.

Figure 3.6 The concrete bollards along this pedestrian route are difficult to distinguish visually from the tarmac surface. Any redundant or broken features should be removed where possible. These bollards no longer serve their original purpose as this area does not have vehicle access. Taller bollards that contrast visually with the background surface would be preferable in this location. A low-cost, short-term option would be to paint the bollards and / or add a reflective band to increase their visibility.

**External ramps and steps** – Ramps and steps in the external environment are key to overcoming natural and manmade changes in level. For all but the smallest change in level (that is less than 300mm), steps as well as ramps should be provided and positioned sufficiently close so that people are aware of the choice of route. Steps and ramps should be measured in detail as part of an access audit, as the dimensions and configuration are critical in ensuring ease of use and safe access. The design, position and detailing of handrails is similarly important.

Figure 3.7 This linear ramp provides direct access to the building entrance. It is wide enough for people to pass each other, has a firm non-slip surface and visually contrasting handrail to one side. The planting box has been designed to support the handrails and form an upstanding edge that contrasts visually with the ramp slope. The ramp could be improved by adding handrails on both sides, extending the handrail at the top and bottom of the ramp and the ends turned under.

Figure 3.8 Temporary ramps should meet the same design criteria as permanent ramps. The ramp to this temporary information facility has been well designed and ensures the venue is accessible to everyone. Because the total change in level is less than 300mm, adjacent steps are not required.

Figure 3.9 Portable ramps should be fit for purpose and if handrails are not possible, due care should be taken to ensure users are confident in their use independently. This should be part of the management process that supports a portable or temporary solution.

Figure 3.10 These external steps have suitable tread and riser dimensions, but the open riser arrangement is a potential trip hazard as well as a source of visual confusion.

Figure 3.11 This fire exit presents several issues; it is stepped, has no handrails and leads on to a gravel path. The 'No Dogs' sign could read 'guide dogs only' to be more inclusive of visually impaired visitors.

Figure 3.12 This ramp and flight of steps are clearly visible within the street environment. The ramp provides a gently inclined route with level landings to overcome a small change in level along the access route. Adding signage indicating the location of lift access to the high-level walkway would help many pedestrians.

**Entrances** – The main building entrance should be audited, together with any alternative entrance points in regular use, whether they are available to the general public or designated as staff-only entrances. Aspects to consider include how easy the entrance is to identify from the approach routes and the suitability of any signage along the routes. Detailed aspects of the entrance doors, lobbies, threshold and surfaces as well as door widths and the use of glazing should all be assessed.

Figure 3.13 This projecting canopy highlights the location of the main entrance within the façade and also provides protection from the weather. Revolving doors are not considered to be best practice and where possible removed and replaced with sliding doors or a draft lobby, if weather and temperature control is an issue.

Figure 3.14 These entrance doors have been designed to blend in with the façade and are likely to be difficult for many people to identify. The access control system is positioned too high and may be beyond the reach of some wheelchair users and people of short stature. Door furniture helps to identify the opening direction if installed intuitively. Pull handles appear on this inward opening door and may cause some confusion.

Figure 3.15 Permanent markings have been applied to highlight the presence of full-height glass in these library entrance doors. The markings are reasonably effective, but restrict visibility unnecessarily through the lower half of the door. To enable people at a range of heights to see and be seen through the doors in both directions, manifestation is recommended at two height ranges, mid-height 850 - 1000mm and at a higher level 1400 - 1600mm.

Figure 3.16 This is a fire exit. Signage should indicate a stepped fire exit to warn building users. This step could be manageable in the event of an evacuation if the step is less than 100mm.

Figure 3.17 The glass gates to this control barrier are barely visible and may present a hazard to people unfamiliar with the environment. The application of markings to highlight the presence of the glass would be beneficial. Changes in floor colour could be used to assist, if layout of features is carefully planned. Barrier gates should also have wide access and sufficient time should be given on opening and closing the security mechanism.

**Doors** – The design, size and position of doors as well as the suitability of handles, locks and other door furniture all influence the usability of every individual door and the building as a whole. All of these aspects should be considered in an audit as well as associated features such as access control systems and powered–operation.

Figure 3.18 This push-pad device activates the powered entrance doors, is positioned clear of the door swing and is easy to identify.

**Reception areas** – Most sites or buildings that permit access by members of the public will have some form of reception, security, box office or information point. Where these are staffed, valuable information about services and any existing barriers to access can be gained from discussions with front-line personnel. The design of any reception desk or counter itself is also important, as is the availability of suitable seating and clear signage.

Figure 3.19 This reception desk is clearly visible from the main entrance doors and includes counters at two heights. The receptionist is clearly visible. There is no knee recess on the customer side to enable wheelchair users to sit close to the counter and sign papers. In the short term, a clipboard has been provided to enable people to sign the visitors' book more easily.

**Horizontal circulation** – This includes the overall layout of routes within a building as well as specific features such as corridors, passageways, aisles and internal lobbies. The width of circulation routes is important, but should be considered in the context of the building type, its function and patterns of use.

**Surfaces and visual contrast** – The characteristics of surface finishes can assist or impede orientation and wayfinding and may significantly affect the ease of passage throughout a building for all users. Characteristics of surface finishes can also influence acoustic conditions and may affect the ease with which people are able to communicate and navigate around a building. Effective visual contrast between surfaces, fixtures and fittings is paramount and can greatly help visually impaired people to differentiate between features. Textured surfaces are useful in providing information for people with visual impairments.

Figure 3.20 The cubicle doors in this washroom provide effective visual contrast with the adjacent floor and wall surfaces.

**Vertical circulation** – Vertical circulation includes ramps, steps, lifts and platform lifts. In buildings that are wholly or partly open to members of the public, but where there are potential physical barriers to access within major circulation routes, an audit is likely to include a consideration as to whether services could be relocated as an alternative to making substantial physical modifications. For example, there may be an opportunity to relocate a customer service desk from the second floor of a three-storey building to the ground floor if there is no lift provided.

Figure 3.21 The nosing of each step on these stairs provides good visual contrast with the tread and riser surfaces. Continuous handrails are provided to both sides of the stair, but they may be difficult for some people to see as the contrast between the floors, the walls and the wooden handrails is insufficient. This can be improved by changing the colour of the wall.

**Sanitary facilities** – The full complement of sanitary facilities should be included in an access audit, not just accessible WC provision. Single-sex toilet areas should be reviewed to assess provision for ambulant disabled people, for people who need more space and to ensure taps and accessories are all clearly visible, within reach and easy to operate. Where provided, baby-changing facilities should be provided separately from single-sex toilet areas and be accessible. Changing Places toilets are becoming more widespread and should be assessed against guidance from the Changing Places Consortium.

Figure 3.22 The visual contrast between fittings and surfaces in this unisex accessible toilet is effective and the overall room size meets current standards. It would be preferable for the toilet paper dispenser to be lowered and for paper hand towels to be provided within reach of the WC. It is essential that the alarm pull cord be released from the fixed support rail as it will not work in this position, and the transfer area should be kept clear.

Figure 3.23 This Changing Places toilet is spacious and well equipped and demonstrates good visual contrast between surfaces and fixtures.

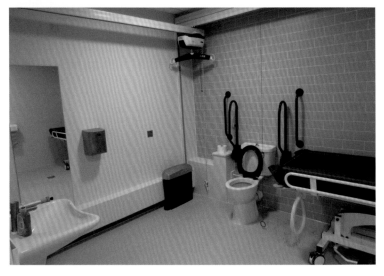

**Activity spaces** – Every building or environment will have activity spaces or rooms for people to meet or use for a specific purpose and these should all be covered by an access audit. In schools, for example, classrooms, assembly halls and libraries should be included in an audit and in theatres, front-of-house facilities, the auditorium and backstage areas should all be covered. Auditors should consider the accessibility of all areas used by customers, visitors, staff, volunteers, students and pupils, performers and any other people using the building.

Figure 3.24 Artwork has been displayed in these purpose-built structures, designed to be accessible. Upstands or contrast on edges would improve the ramps and reduce the risk of trip hazard.

Figure 3.25 Access to these height-adjustable rotary washing lines has been carefully considered. The concrete path has been extended sufficiently to provide residents year-round level access to each individual washing line while preserving as much of the lawn as possible but ensure the width of access routes is sufficient.

**Wayfinding, information and signs** – These are all essential components that contribute to the accessibility of a site or building. The overall system of wayfinding includes the inherent legibility of a site or building, the presence of landmark features to aid orientation, guidance systems and signage.

Figure 3.26 This information sign highlights the key facilities at each floor level and incorporates symbols and directional arrows. The dark text and symbols contrast visually with the signboard, which is a good feature, but there is minimal contrast between the signboard and mounting surface and the size of the text means that the sign needs to be read at close range.

Figure 3.27 Information signs should be placed in logical positions where they are easily visible as part of the approach to a feature. Information in these signs would be better positioned on angled signboards mounted on the landing balustrade where they could be read at close range by people at different heights. In their current location, people need to stand on the lower stairs to be close enough to read the signs – this is potentially hazardous and inappropriate for many building users.

Figure 3.28 This exhibit sign includes pictograms as well as large text and embossed tactile controls. It is mounted horizontally at a height to suit people who are seated or standing. The controls are recessed however and would be better on the flush surface.

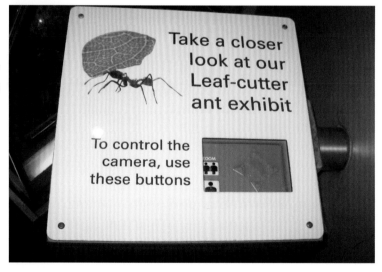

Figure 3.29 Information is conveyed simply but very clearly in this sign, which is distinctive and prominently positioned.

**Communication systems** – Communication systems may include door entry systems, hearing and speech enhancement systems (for example induction loops, infrared and radio systems), public address systems and visual display units, the availability of communication support services (for example British Sign Language / English interpreters, lipspeakers, speech-to-text display) and audio description. As well as checking for the presence of equipment and corresponding signage, it is important to establish whether staff are familiar with using the system and that procedures are in place to monitor and test equipment.

**Acoustics** – The acoustic characteristics of a building should be assessed for their impact on the usability of the building and its spaces. Acoustics in a building can be affected by the size, shape and proportions of rooms and by the relative location of quiet and noisy areas, as well as by the characteristics of surface finishes. Equipment such as hearing enhancement systems may also be considered an integral component of the acoustic environment, or as part of the building's communication systems, as discussed above.

**Switches and controls** – Where switches and controls are available for the individual operation of equipment or services in a building, they should be readily identifiable, positioned within reach and easy to use. An access audit should include observations of switches and controls as well as any associated instructions and labelling.

**Lighting** – The effects of natural and artificial lighting within a site or building can greatly affect accessibility by creating a potential barrier in its own right, for example by presenting a source of glare, or by affecting the perception of other building features, for example poor illumination to a flight of stairs. Lighting issues should be considered as an integral component of the accessibility of physical features such as circulation routes, activity rooms and means of escape, but also in terms of the lighting installation itself, including issues such as luminaire type, position and controls.

Figure 3.30 The seating area in front of this large window can be difficult to see from the internal approach route because the bright daylight causes the seating to appear in silhouette. The use of window blinds and adjustable internal lighting is likely to reduce glare and provide a more even level of illumination to the interior.

**Building management** – The way a building or venue is managed encompasses a wide range of issues including practical tasks such as general maintenance and the servicing of equipment. It also includes the way in which staff interact with building users, the manner in which services are delivered, the availability of auxiliary aids and services and the development of policies and staff training.

Figure 3.31 This accessible toilet is being used as a temporary store, rendering it entirely unusable. This is not acceptable under any circumstances.

Figure 3.32 Mobility assistance is available on this large campus to enable disabled visitors to travel between venues.

**Means of escape** – The means and route of escape from a site or building in an emergency is equally important as the route of entry and should be fully considered in any audit. Issues to consider include the suitability and operation of alarm systems, the identification and accessibility of exit routes and evacuation procedures. There is likely also to be a link with building management and staff training issues.

Figure 3.33 A refuge area is provided on this stair landing and is clearly signed. A means of two-way communication should be provided to enable a person waiting in the refuge to communicate directly with the person organising the evacuation. The need for an evacuation chair should be discussed with building management.

## 3.3 Survey equipment

The audit survey involves a range of recording techniques, including quantitative measurement and observational assessment. On-site measurements of physical features are essential to the audit survey for comparison with current best practice design guidance.

Key equipment for quantitative measurement includes the following:

**Measuring tape** – A tape is an absolute essential for any audit. A two-metre tape is often sufficient, although a five-metre tape will suffice for the majority of audits. Electronic tapes are available that display and 'announce' the measurement, which may assist some auditors.

**Gradient measure** – An instrument for measuring the gradient of a surface, for example a ramp, path or floor surface, is an invaluable time-saving tool. While some gradients can be calculated (by dividing the length of the ramp or surface by the height of the rise), it is not always easy to accurately measure the rise, particularly for internal surfaces. A tool such as a gradient measure incorporates a spirit level, an adjustable graduated 'leg' and a table for reading the gradients for each numbered value on the leg.

Figure 3.34 Using a two-metre tape to take detailed measurements of the steps.

Figure 3.35 Using a gradient measure to measure the gradient of a ramp.

**Door pressure gauge** – A range of instruments is available for measuring door–opening and closing forces, but the quality and consequently the accuracy of the equipment can vary significantly. As door pressure levels need to be verified with a reasonable degree of accuracy (± two newtons), a good-quality gauge is recommended. Plunger-type models enable doors to be pushed as well as pulled open in order to assess the opening force, which is useful for double-swing doors without pull handles.

Figure 3.36 Measuring door pressure levels using a door pressure gauge.

**Light meters** – Light meters can be used to measure the level of illumination of, for example, a reception counter, a work surface, corridor or lift interior. However, levels of illumination can be greatly affected by the direction, intensity and nature of natural light sources and weather conditions, which may distort light meter readings. An assessment of lighting in an environment should in any case take into account the quality of light, colour rendering, luminaire position and potential glare, in addition to the level of illuminance. In this case, it is often better to make an observational qualitative assessment of all these issues, rather than to focus on a single quantitative measurement that could vary considerably at different times of the day. For further information on measuring light meters, refer to the Chartered Institute of Building Services Engineers (CIBSE) guidance.

## 3.4 Observational assessment

Many aspects of access auditing relate to features in the built environment that cannot be measured using scientific instruments. Clearly, a different approach is needed in these circumstances, as the assessment is observational rather than objective.

**Camera and video recorder** – A digital camera is an incredibly useful tool for most auditors. Photographs not only provide useful illustrations in audit reports, but are also an invaluable reminder of features in the building or environment after the audit survey is completed.

Video recorders are not essential, but can be used to advantage to record information for the auditor to later review, and can be particularly useful in recording the movement of people in an environment. A video recorder can also be used to provide a 'virtual' walk-through audit, complete with running commentary, for a client to view as a form of audit record.

With any type of camera or video recorder, the permission of the client or building owner should be sought before any photographs are taken. This is particularly important in public buildings where security, confidentiality and public protection may otherwise be compromised.

**Visual contrast** – An adequate degree of visual contrast between adjacent surfaces, or fixtures and fittings and the background they are viewed against, is important to enable people with a visual impairment to differentiate between surfaces, to locate items such as door handles and to identify potential obstructions. Visual contrast is established by comparing the Light Reflectance Values (LRVs) of different surfaces. The LRV represents how much useful light is reflected from a surface, with higher value LRVs indicating a higher level of reflectance. LRVs can be measured using a spectrophotometer or hand-held colorimeter. Spectrophotometers are more sophisticated, but are laboratory based and clearly not suitable for on-site assessments. Hand-held colorimeters provide a means of assessing LRVs on site but are limited in application, are not suitable for measuring curved surfaces or gloss finishes and are not currently widely available.

Of more relevance to access auditors is an observational assessment of the degree of visual contrast, taking into account the effects of the ambient lighting. As the effectiveness of visual contrast is predominantly affected by the difference in LRV, an effective assessment can be made of the degree of contrast by converting the view into a monochrome image. Most products such as paint, now contain information about their LRV and this can be used when specifying. However, the LRV of a product is variable depending on the environment it is in.

Practical ways to achieve this are by photocopying a colour photograph to produce a grey-scale image, by taking a black and white photograph or by converting a digital colour photograph into grey scale. Each of these relatively low-tech methods provides an image of an environment which may be easier to assess for adequate visual contrast than a view of the full-colour original environment. The effects of reflections from strong lighting may also be more apparent in a monochrome image.

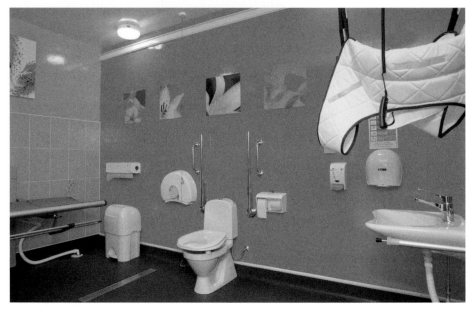

Figure 3.37 and 3.38 Converting a colour image into grey scale can make it easier to assess the effectiveness of visual contrast between surfaces and fixtures. But beware of increasingly sophisticated software that may automatically attempt to enhance or alter the original image and consequently give a false impression of the visual environment.

**Lighting** – Although lighting levels can be measured (see Light meters in previous section), it is important that a holistic assessment of the quality and effects of light in an environment is made, taking into account the overall levels of illumination, the position, direction, intensity and nature of light sources and the influence of natural light.

It is important to identify existing and potential sources of reflection and glare, as these can be a significant source of confusion for visually impaired people. Similarly, where lighting (either natural or artificial) may cause shadows, or strong pools of light and dark, these should be identified as they may conceal a potential obstacle or be perceived as a change in level or direction.

The positioning of key objects, signs or people in relation to light sources (including natural and artificial light) can have a significant impact on the accessibility of an environment. For example, a receptionist could appear as a silhouette if positioned in front of a window, which would make it very difficult for a person who communicates using lipreading and therefore needs to see the receptionist's face clearly.

**Acoustics** – A well-designed acoustic environment can greatly benefit hearing impaired and visually impaired people as well as providing a pleasant environment for other building users. Hearing impaired people who have some residual hearing find it easier to communicate if background noise levels are kept to a minimum. Visually impaired people may use different sounds to navigate within an environment, for example by differentiating between the sound of footsteps on different floor surfaces and locating a lift by the sound of the arrival bell.

A number of observations of the environment and its facilities should be made during the audit survey to assess the likely impact of the quality of the acoustic environment. These include the relative location of areas in the building which may be a potential source of noise intrusion. For example, is the reception desk far enough away from the external doors to avoid communications being impaired by external traffic noise? The nature and range of surface finishes in an environment provides an indication of the degree of reverberation. An area with all hard surfaces, for example a marble or tiled floor, plastered walls and ceilings and steel or timber furniture is likely to be highly reverberant and susceptible to high noise levels, which could be generated by a small number of people in the room. Softer surfaces such as carpets, mineral tile ceilings, heavy curtains and upholstered furniture all help to absorb sound reverberation and are likely to help reduce background noise, but may inhibit the identification of sounds that could aid navigation.

**Wayfinding** – The ease with which people navigate around an environment depends largely on two factors. One is the 'readability' of the environment or building itself, namely how logically the spaces and functions are arranged and the use of landmark features. The other is by following a specific guidance system, for example maps and guides, or a system of signage which has been applied to the environment. Signage could include visual as well as tactile information. Audio information and audio description can also be used as part of a wayfinding system. Often, a combination of these factors is involved, particularly in large or complex environments.

The overall 'readability' of an environment can only be judged by experiencing the building or site first hand and by considering the experience of other building users. It is often easier for an auditor to assess wayfinding characteristics when visiting a building or environment for the first time, as the experience will then be comparable to that of other unfamiliar visitors. Auditors assessing a building they know well will need to take a deliberate step back in order to consider how the environment will be perceived by first-time or unfamiliar visitors.

Maps, guides and signage can all be assessed for their individual accessibility by considering, for example, visual contrast, text size and style, the use of symbols and general legibility. The position of wayfinding information is also critical to its usability, and an assessment should be made of the suitability of the location, height and relationship to other fixtures or elements of the environment. Of equal importance is the relevance and effectiveness of the guidance system in enabling building users to locate key facilities and exit routes.

**Olfactory features** – Features in an environment that can be detected by a person's sense of smell can contribute to the system of wayfinding in an environment, whether by design or by default. For example, the deliberate use of fragrant planting adjacent to an entrance can help identify the main route into a building. Cooking smells from the kitchen or carvery in a large pub or hotel may help to identify the location of the restaurant seating area – this is more likely to be an unavoidable consequence of the function of a particular area, but nonetheless a potentially valuable one for a person using senses other than vision to navigate around an environment.

## 3.5 Data recording

Various methods of recording survey information are available and their use depends on individual preference and client requirements. They include taking notes, annotating plans, drawing sketches, completing checklists or a blank pre-prepared table, the use of a dictation machine or dictation to a note-taker, or entering data directly into a laptop or hand-held device.

**Checklists** – Pre-prepared checklists are a useful auditing tool and a great asset on site, particularly for less experienced auditors. Checklists provide a prompt to the types of feature to look for and, if suitably structured, guide the auditor on a logical sequence in relation to the site or building.

The checklists included in the appendix to this publication are suitable for use in a range of public buildings and cover the various elements of a building and its setting. Many of the individual checklists also suit elements of workplace and other environments. Checklists can be printed or photocopied for use on site, making them equally suitable for a large complex building, or multiple buildings on a single site. Individual checklists can be reproduced several times to record multiple elements of a particular feature, where necessary.

Checklists are regarded as an auditing tool and should not be used in isolation as a report format. They are an effective means of gathering information on site, but require interpretation in order to be of benefit to a client. The data gathered in a checklist requires explanation and should be set out alongside recommendations so that the client is armed with sufficient guidance to progress. Audit data can be set out in either narrative or tabular format, as described in chapter 4.

**Pre-prepared tables** – Blank pre-prepared tables can be used to record site measurements and observations. This method is particularly useful if the audit report is to be set out in tabular format as it is easy for data to be transferred directly to a computer. If the tables are set up and structured in a logical way, this method of data recording can help to ensure that a logical route is followed around the site or building.

**Ratings** – Ratings tables typically comprise tick boxes relating to a series of questions. The questions generally prompt a yes / no response, but offer minimal scope for recording the context of any particular feature. Ratings reports may incorporate a scoring system, which some clients find useful for statistical analysis. This type of report is unlikely to provide adequate detailed recommendations to enable clients to fully consider the range of adjustments that need to be made.

**Information technology** – The use of computers and hand-held devices offer the opportunity to use pre-prepared databases and templates, either prepared in house by the auditor, or purchased as one of many available ready-made auditing software products. Ready-made auditing software typically includes a series of standard questions relating to, for example, features of the building, plus one or more standard responses, including recommendations for improvements. Such systems can be beneficial to the auditor by providing a question or prompt to measure or observe features of a site in a structured order. Inputting data directly into a computer or hand-held device may also save a lot of time which can otherwise be spent transferring handwritten or dictated notes into electronic format. Despite the benefits, a word of caution is required here. Pre-prepared databases pose a number of limitations for the auditor and can significantly restrict the ability to record non-standard issues, multiple recommendations and to describe a feature in context. It may also be difficult to modulate recommendations to suit different clients, for example a recommendation to overcome a change in floor level in a village hall with limited financial resources is likely to differ from recommendations for the same scenario in a large corporation with substantial turnover. If pre-prepared databases or templates are used, great care should be taken to ensure that all issues are considered in the context of the building / service and that the context for any observations and recommendations is fully considered and recorded.

## 3.6 User participation

One of the most effective ways of finding out about an environment or building and its occupants is talking to regular users, including customers, staff, patients, pupils, students, and so on. For businesses and organisations, this may also include the business or building owner, the property or facilities manager, reception and customer service staff, health and safety representatives, equal opportunities officers and human resources personnel. Where the building being audited is a community-based premises, for example a village hall, the management committee, volunteers and representatives of user groups are likely to be able to contribute invaluable information in relation to the use of the premises and any existing problems that have been encountered. Existing building occupants are often able to report on problems encountered by service users and on any adjustments that can readily be made to ensure services and facilities are accessible.

As well as discussing how the environment is used, building users may be able to report on any existing links with local access groups and local authority access officers. Advice on making improvements to the building or any services delivered from it may have already been given, and this is often worth noting, particularly where the work has already been or is in the process of being implemented. Where adjustments have already been implemented as a response to duties under equality legislation, these should be noted.

Figure 3.39 Consultation with building users can provide invaluable insight into the accessibility of a site or building and the services provided from it.

Once an access audit has been undertaken and a client is formulating an access plan or strategy, the continued participation of users is paramount. The auditor may or may not be involved at this post-audit stage, and it may be more typical for the client to facilitate effective consultation and the participation of service users as part of the decision-making process, prior to the implementation of improvements. User consultation should be inclusive and involve a broad range of existing and / or prospective building or service users.

Depending on the site or building type, it may be appropriate to facilitate formal consultation during the audit process with a local access group or focus group, as well as staff, volunteers, regular visitors and user representatives. This is particularly relevant for major public buildings and for projects where an audit is being undertaken as a precursor to a substantial refurbishment or redevelopment programme.

Consultation may be initiated by either the client or the auditor. If a client is, for example, a local authority, it is likely that there are already established links with a local user group, which can be developed to engage views on a particular project. Where there are no established links, the client or auditor may be required to initiate contact with an existing user group or invite representatives from local or national organisations to formulate a project-specific focus group. It is important in all cases that the user group includes members with a broad range of experience of disability as well as members who represent different user categories, such as staff, visitors, volunteers, customers and so on.

It is recommended that specific terms of reference for consultation are established at the outset, to ensure that all parties understand the aims and objectives of the process. Suggested items for incorporation into terms of reference are given in the inset box on page 40.

## Terms of reference for user group / focus group consultation

**Aims and objectives** – It is essential that the aims and objectives of the consultation process are clarified for all parties concerned. These are likely to include the following:

• To include building users in the process of redevelopment of an environment / service and to keep local people informed of developments.
• To explore views on specific aspects such as physical features, management and operational issues, communications and interpretation.
• For the client organisation to increase their awareness and understanding of user needs and of how the environment / service can be made more accessible and inclusive.

**Managing expectations** – The consultation process will undoubtedly generate a broad range of comments and recommendations for improving the environment or service in question. However, it may not be practical operationally, or financially viable, to act on every point of view or to implement every recommendation, and this should be acknowledged at the outset. In order to successfully manage expectations, it is useful to provide as much background information as possible about the project, including information such as budget, potential sources of external funding, timescales for implementation and other expenditure commitments so that members of the consultation group are aware of the context for their recommendations.

**Level and type of advice** – Depending on the nature of the environment / service being audited and the progress of any redevelopment proposals, the level of advice generated or required as part of the consultation process may vary considerably. For example, if the consultation process revolves around the audit of an existing public building where the client wishes to formulate a project brief for substantial redevelopment, it is likely that general rather than specific recommendations for physical modifications will be discussed as part of the consultation process. Specific recommendations in this context, such as installing a lift in a particular location, may stifle creativity in terms of the overall redevelopment. General recommendations, or options for improvement, may be more appropriate in this scenario. In other situations, for example an audit of an existing museum that is planning to improve display and interpretation material, the outcome of the consultation process could be much more specific and include detailed recommendations on the production of printed, tactile, audio and virtual media.

**Reporting and recording procedures** – Clear lines of communication should be established, alongside responsibilities for recording and disseminating information to all parties. Minutes of meetings and a record of issues discussed during site visits should be distributed to everyone involved in the consultation process. Alternative formats such as large print, Braille and audio should be produced to suit individual need.

**Payment of fees and expenses** – Travel expenses should be offered to group members for attendance at site visits and meetings. Where the budget allows, a fee for group members' time should also be offered.

**Meeting arrangements** – The number, frequency, duration and timing of proposed meetings should be clarified and, where possible, agreed to suit the availability and particular requirements of group members. The venue selected for meetings should be accessible and equipment such as induction loops made available, if required. Access requirements can be gathered from attendees as they register their interest and should be actioned prior to the meeting.

**Site visits** – Where the consultation process involves the audit of an existing environment, it is clearly advantageous to arrange a site visit, wherever possible. This should be planned and arrangements made to facilitate access by group members, where required. If a part or whole of the site cannot be accessed by some members, particular features could be illustrated or described in order to facilitate discussion at a meeting held in an alternative accessible location.

**Communication support** – Arrangements should be made in advance of any meetings or site visits to provide appropriate communication support to meet the needs of individual group members. This may include the provision of British Sign Language (BSL) / English interpreters, deaf-blind interpreters and communicator guides, lipspeakers, note-takers or speech-to-text reporters. Equipment such as an induction loop may also be required.

## 3.7 Building management

The way a building or site is managed can have a significant effect on the accessibility of services and facilities. Poor building management can render a potentially physically accessible environment inaccessible and may impact on all building users.

Building management covers a range of practical issues including caretaking, cleaning, equipment servicing, repairs and maintenance as well as customer service and operational issues. It also covers staff equality awareness training and systems and procedures for implementing and monitoring good practice. The nature and extent of the tasks associated with these issues will vary significantly between, for example, a small community hall and a large campus-style hospital, but are equally important to both organisations.

The effectiveness of a building management system can be partly determined by an observation of the building fabric, namely the overall quality of decoration, cleanliness and whether there are any significant repairs outstanding. However, to gain a sufficient understanding of how the building or site is managed, it will be necessary, as part of the audit survey, to communicate with the person or people responsible for this aspect of work. Discussions should be held as part of the audit survey with property managers, caretakers, cleaners or maintenance engineers, wherever possible, to gauge the general approach to building / site management, how quickly repairs are undertaken and whether regular checks are made of particular equipment such as hearing enhancement systems, fire alarms and emergency lighting, platform lifts and so on.

Response procedures to alarms and call bells are considered to be part of the overall building management system and should be discussed with staff and building users. For example, who is responsible for responding to the assistance alarm in the WC and do they have appropriate training? Is there a procedure for responding promptly to a door bell or 'assistance required' bell so that people are not kept waiting? In some circumstances, it may be appropriate as part of an audit survey to activate call bells and alarms without prior warning to witness the response first hand. However, this is not always appropriate and is inadvisable in the case of emergency alarms.

It is also important to identify as part of the audit process the range and nature of existing building management solutions which have been implemented to overcome physical barriers to access. This might include, for example, the provision of assistance to use a temporary ramp, before construction of a permanent ramp and steps to an existing building entrance. Providing help in a shop to retrieve goods displayed at high level or in an inaccessible location is another example, and likely to be typical of many retail establishments. There may be instances where a service is offered to members of the public in an alternative way, such as the provision of a telephone ordering and home delivery service for goods otherwise purchased from a high street shop. Similarly, where a potential physical barrier is identified during the audit process, recommendations should include not only options to remove or physically alter the barrier, but identify where there is also the potential to provide a service in an alternative way or in an alternative location, if this is relevant to the client.

# 4.0 Report writing

## 4.1 A communication tool

Preparing an effective report of an audit is key to communicating the survey findings and recommendations to a client. A written or video report documents the accessibility of the site, building and its services at a particular moment in time, and may constitute supporting evidence in future cases of alleged discrimination.

An audit report may be the only form of communication between an auditor and a client, for example when the client is a large corporate body and the audit has been commissioned by one department, but the report circulated to several affected departments. It is unlikely, in this scenario, that the auditor would have the opportunity to meet and discuss the audit process and outcomes with everybody likely to see the report. Clearly then, it is paramount that the document carries a full explanation of the purpose of the audit and detailed recommendations that enable the client to move towards the preparation of an access action plan and the implementation of access improvements.

Ideally, an audit report will constitute part of the audit feedback process to the client. Wherever possible, direct communication, presentations, a debriefing or action planning meeting will also be held with the client to fully explain the outcomes of the audit and discuss how best the client can move forward.

In any scenario, the clarity, quality and effectiveness of the written audit report is paramount.

**Report style and presentation**

The basic characteristics of an effective audit report are a logical and clear structure, well-written, informative and usable content and good presentation.

The method of presentation can have a significant impact on the legibility and usefulness of an audit report. The style and format adopted will depend on the particular requirements of the client, and should be tailored to meet their particular needs – there is no 'one size fits all'.

Audit reports will typically comprise a printed document but may also be transmitted electronically to a client. Electronic copies of the report provide the opportunity for adjustment of the font size and style to suit particular end users and for the document to be read using specialist screen or data-reading software. Reports can also be integrated with existing building management systems and be easily updated when improvements are implemented.

The categories set out in the inset box provide a guide to the type and range of information typically included in access audit reports. The list should be tailored to individual audits.

## Guidelines for audit report structure

**Title page** – The title page should clearly identify the title of the report, the site or building and / or parts of these subject to audit, the report author (whether an individual or company) and a document date. The name of the client / person who commissioned the audit may also be included.

**Contents page** – The use of page numbers throughout the document and a contents page make it much easier for the reader to immediately understand the layout of the report and to locate specific information.

**Introduction** – This section will typically set the context for the commission and may include brief details of the site, building or services being audited.

**Client brief / scope of audit** – The scope of the audit will reflect the client brief; it will establish which parts of the building and service are to be included in the audit and any exclusions. It may also include specific reasons for carrying out the audit, such as in connection with a funding application. As described in chapter two Commissioning an access audit, the brief should indicate particular requirements in terms of output, for example the type and format of the report and any requirement for specific optional information such as priority ratings, categories for recommendations and cost bands.

**Audit details** – The site and / or building name and address, date of the audit survey and name of the auditor should be clearly recorded.

**Description of site / building and functions** – It is useful to provide a description of the site and / or building being audited, including information such as ownership, approximate size / area, number of floors, type of construction and age. If the building or any feature is listed, this should be noted, as it is likely to affect the nature of any recommendations. An explanation should be included of how the site or building is used, whether some areas are restricted to staff-only access, and whether access is available to members of the public, as this information is key to the audit process, particularly in the context of various duties under equality legislation.

**Legislative context** – Given that the majority of access audits are commissioned in the context of equality legislation, a section setting out the background to the Equality Act and the key duties, as relevant to the site, building or client in question, is particularly important.

**Criteria for assessment** – The benchmark by which observations and recommendations are made should be clearly set out and is likely to comprise a list of documents including Approved Document Part M, Approved Document K, BS 8300:2009+A1:2010, relevant local design guides, other publications and client requirements for inclusive access.

**Explanation of priorities and categories** – Where the client requires recommendations to be prioritised and / or categorised, the basis for defining these should be clearly set out.

**Disclaimer** – It is advisable to clearly set out the limitations of the audit report. The Equality Act is not compliance based and not prescriptive in its requirements; therefore, clients should be advised that adherence to the recommendations in the report does not provide immunity from prosecution under the Act. However, disclaimers are of limited practical value and anyone proposing to rely on one should seek legal advice.

**Summary (or executive summary)** – It is useful, particularly for lengthy reports, to include a summary highlighting the key issues in the audit. The summary can be used to provide a brief overview of the current accessibility of the site / building and to identify significant recommendations.

**Main body of audit** – This is likely to be the most substantial part of the audit report and will record the details of the audit survey and set out recommendations for potential improvements. The way in which this information is set out is likely to depend on the client's requirements and the size and complexity of the building. Some examples of different report formats are discussed on the pages to follow, including narrative and tabular reports.

**Appendices** – These can be used to set out supplementary information such as design guidance, general recommendations, photographs (if not included in the main body of the report), site or building plans, a copy of an organisation's access policy or other supporting documents, a list of useful contacts and a bibliography.

**Use of language** – The appropriate use of language is important, and an audit report provides the opportunity for the auditor to demonstrate good practice. The social model of disability supports the use of the terms 'disabled person' or 'disabled people', as distinct from 'the disabled' or 'a person or people with disabilities', which are not good practice. The word 'accessible' is regarded as a more inclusive term and preferred to 'disabled' when describing features such as an accessible WC, accessible or designated parking bay, accessible lift, accessible route, and so on.

Terms to be avoided when making recommendations include any phrase that implies or suggests that a particular feature 'complies' with the Equality Act. Service providers, employers and others may indeed comply with their respective duties under the Act, by making reasonable adjustments in relation to services and employment practices. This would be an appropriate use of the term 'comply'. However, the Equality Act does not include prescriptive guidance on the design or provision of building features and it would be misleading to suggest that the provision of, for example, an accessible WC or a ramp at a specific gradient, would 'comply' with the Act. The provision of a particular physical feature does not in itself ensure or necessarily demonstrate 'compliance' with the Act.

The use of clear English throughout the report is paramount as this will greatly improve legibility and clarity for all readers. The use of jargon should be avoided, particularly for non-technical clients.

## 4.2 Report formats

There are many different formats for audit reports and the use of any one particular format will depend on the nature and type of site or building and on the needs of the client. No one type of format will suit all clients or all audits – a format should be developed that communicates the outcome of the audit most effectively to the client.

Two of the more commonly used report formats are described below – these are categorised as narrative and tabular reports. An example of each type of audit report is included in chapter five Access audit extracts.

### Narrative reports

Narrative audit reports are characterised by detailed descriptive text. The report style is typically lengthy and includes a clear description of existing features, an explanation as to why particular features may present a potential barrier and detailed recommendations for potential improvements. Narrative reports are an effective way to discuss particular features in the overall context of the building. This style of report is generally more readable than structured tabular reports and may therefore be more suitable for non-technical clients. Such reports are usually more suited to smaller sites or buildings.

Narrative reports also provide a suitable format for walk-and-talk audits, where an auditor undertakes a site survey with the client, discusses key issues while on site and prepares a brief written record of the visit, summarising key points.

**Tabular reports**

Tabular reports, as their name suggests, comprise a series of tables used to set out and structure information. In tabular reports, text and descriptions are generally more succinct than in narrative reports, but should still be sufficiently detailed to provide usable information for the client.

Tabular reports can be used for any size of building, but are particularly suitable for larger sites or buildings where a narrative report would be too long and unwieldy. Data can be easily extracted from tabular reports, as long as the information is set out in a logical order and is clearly referenced – this may be an advantage if a client is collating information in a particular category, for example surface finishes across a number of different floor levels.

When undertaking the audit survey, pre-prepared tables can be used to record site measurements and observations. This method of data recording can help to ensure a logical route is followed around the site or building, if the tables are set up in a structured way.

Tables can easily be expanded to incorporate particular information required by the client, for example priority ratings, categories and cost bands. Where audit reports are provided in electronic format, clients can import data into their own database and add columns to record progress, cost and any other relevant details.

## 4.3 Establishing the legislative context

Many audits are carried out in response to duties placed on clients by equality legislation – historically this was the Disability Discrimination Acts and currently the Equality Act 2010. It is important for auditors to provide clear information about the relevant sections of applicable legislation and how they might relate to a particular client. For example, if an audit is carried out for a high street retailer, it is likely the client will need information on Part five (for staff areas) and Part three (for public areas) of the Act; an organisation with employees, but not providing a service to the general public, will most likely only need information on Part five; membership associations will need information on Part seven as well as Part five (for staff), and schools will need information on Part six as well as Part five (for staff) and Part three in relation to services the school provides direct to people who are not pupils or students.

However, the role of the access auditor or consultant is not that of a legal advisor. There may be situations when it is not clear how the Equality Act affects the client. In such cases, it is important to recommend that clients seek appropriate legal advice.

It is also important to be clear about the limitations of the guidance contained within the report. An access audit is not a legal requirement, but is widely acknowledged to be a valuable part of the process of implementing improvements to buildings and services in the context of equality legislation.

It should also be made clear, through the use of a disclaimer clause in the report, that acting on the recommendations of the report does not guarantee 'compliance' with equality legislation.

The use of timescales and priorities must be appropriate to the circumstances and agreed with the client in advance. If a priority highlights works that are required within a year, the report needs to make it clear why this is so and who has made the decision. The client's duty is to make reasonable adjustments to ensure disabled people are not discriminated against unjustifiably. The reasonable adjustment might be to provide the service by reasonable alternative means, and may require no physical alterations.

It is the client's responsibility to develop an access strategy / plan and to act upon it. The audit report and the recommendations and priorities contained within it will help this process. The incorrect use of priorities and lack of clarity as to how they relate to equality legislation may result in clients carrying out expensive and inappropriate works. Priorities should distinguish where different parts of the Equality Act apply in relation to the premises and services. A feature identified as a significant barrier may be a high priority if the area is public; however, if the area is restricted to employees and it does not present a barrier to any of them, then making an adjustment would only be required as a matter of good practice.

## 4.4 Criteria for assessment and design guidance

To establish validity for observations and recommendations made in the audit, it is important to set a benchmark by which existing features are assessed. As previously discussed, the Equality Act provides no specific design or dimensional guidance in relation to physical features. The Act sets out duties to make reasonable adjustments for disabled people, but does not stipulate what the adjustments should be and does not set down any specific design criteria. The documents described on pages 50 to 52 provide the basis for establishing minimum requirements for features in and around buildings and should be referenced in any audit. Also relevant are the best practice documents listed in the *Appendix* under *Publications*.

## Building regulations

**England and Wales** – In England and Wales, building design and construction are governed by the building regulations. These regulations comprise a series of requirements for specific purposes: health and safety, energy conservation, prevention of contamination of water and the welfare and convenience of persons in or about buildings.

Building regulations are supported by Approved Documents that give practical guidance with respect to the regulations. While their use is not mandatory – and the requirements of regulations can be met in other ways – Approved Documents are used as a benchmark by building control authorities and approved inspectors. *Approved Document M: Access to and use of Buildings (2013 edition)* (AD M) includes technical guidance on providing access to and within buildings. The 2013 edition of AD M is the 2004 edition incorporating 2010 and 2013 amendments.

Following the transfer of power for making building regulations to the Welsh Ministers on 31 December 2011, changes to building regulations and associated guidance in either England or Wales will relate only to the country in which the changes are made. The existing building regulations and Approved Documents will apply in both countries until changes are made and new guidance issued.

**Scotland** – In Scotland, access requirements are integrated across the building regulations. Practical guidance on meeting the provisions of the building regulations is available in the 2011 Technical Handbooks, available in two volumes: *Domestic buildings and Non-domestic buildings*. Each document has seven sections covering structure, fire, environment, safety, noise, energy and sustainability.

**Northern Ireland** – In Northern Ireland, Part R of the Building Regulations (NI) covers access to and use of buildings, and is supported by Technical Booklet R: 2006. Fire safety is covered in Part E and supported by Technical Booklet E: 2005.

The provisions in AD M, the Technical Handbooks and Technical Booklets represent minimum standards. It is preferable, in many circumstances, to consider going beyond these standards to meet best practice guidelines.

## BS 8300:2009+A1:2010 Design of buildings and their approaches to meet the needs of disabled people - Code of practice

BS 8300 provides comprehensive guidance relating to access to buildings for disabled people. The standard provides detailed guidance on good practice for the design of a range of building types, including workplace and public buildings. Although generally applying to new buildings, BS 8300 provides useful guidance and dimensional criteria that can be used to assess the accessibility of existing buildings. The recommendations apply to car-parking provision, setting-down points and garaging, access routes to and around all buildings, and entrances to and interiors of new buildings. BS 8300 includes commentary which provides a context and rationale for the design guidance. Management and maintenance issues are incorporated in recognition that these play an essential part in the delivery of accessible services and facilities to disabled people.

Many of the design recommendations in BS 8300, which was first published in 2001, were based for the first time on ergonomic research commissioned in 1997 and 2001 by the Department of the Environment, Transport and the Regions. Amendments to the standard were made in 2005 to cover door-closing forces and visual contrast. Further additions were made to the 2009 edition, including guidance on the provision of Changing Places toilet facilities, guidance on using Light Reflectance Values to assess visual contrast, information on the slip potential characteristics of floor finishes and amendments to space allowances data.

Reference to BS 8300 as part of the audit process is particularly valuable where features of a site or building are not otherwise covered by AD M (England and Wales), the Technical Handbooks (Scotland) or Technical Booklets (Northern Ireland). These supporting documents to the relevant building regulations and standards only cover features that can be monitored through the building control process. BS 8300 has a much wider remit and covers features of an environment that are key to accessibility but do not come within the remit of the building control authorities and approved inspectors. A few examples of this include the suitability of floor finishes, the detailed design of signage, and the height of shelving and reception counters.

## BS 9999:2008 Code of practice for fire safety in the design, management and use of buildings

BS 9999 provides comprehensive guidance and recommendations on the design, management and use of buildings in the context of fire safety. Fundamental to the guidance is the understanding that buildings and features in them will be managed, maintained and tested throughout their lifetime and that staff will be adequately trained to put into practice the procedures necessary to bring about the safe evacuation of all occupants.

The guidance in BS 9999 covers all practical planning issues pertinent to the layout and detailed design of buildings from a fire safety point of view, but also provides comprehensive guidance on the management aspects of fire safety, including evacuation strategies, fire training and communications. These management priorities reflect the overriding principles of the UK fire safety legislation, which are to reduce the risk of fire and to ensure people can escape safely in the event of a fire. Legislation requires the person (or people) responsible for managing a building to ensure the safety of everyone who uses it as well as those in the immediate vicinity.

The *Appendix* includes a list of publications, many of which provide design guidance and best practice advice on the provision of accessible facilities and services. Some documents provide general advice, applicable to a range of public buildings, while others provide specific advice on particular features or building types.

Some larger organisations, notably local authorities, publish in-house design guides to support a practical approach to inclusive design. Many such guides are developed in partnership with local access groups and set a benchmark that often goes beyond the minimum provisions of national guidance. Grant-making bodies sometimes have their own standards and criteria. While such design guides are unlikely to be mandatory, they are produced and published in order to promote best practice in inclusive design in a particular area. Where such guides exist and are relevant, they should form part of the benchmark criteria.

There will be occasions when a particular physical feature is not covered in design guidance and the basis for recommending change is not clearly defined. An example of this might be the provision of washing facilities for prayer preparation. There is very little design guidance available relating to the layout and detailing of accessible washing facilities for prayer preparation, although they should be provided in both the male and female washing facilities of relevant buildings. Dimensional and other design criteria in this scenario are likely to be derived from an understanding of the spatial requirements, transfer arrangements, reach ranges, the use of suitable surface finishes and visual contrast covered by existing design guidance for other similar features. These should be applied logically in the context of the particular building being audited.

There may also be instances where a feature is provided in a building which does not accord with published design guidance, but has been provided for a specific purpose and should be retained in its existing configuration. An example of this might be an accessible WC facility in a large primary school which achieves the minimum overall room dimensions, but has been equipped with sanitaryware and handrails that do not accord with the layout in AD M. In fact the sanitaryware and handrails in this example have been positioned to meet the specific needs of a disabled pupil and should clearly not be altered as long as they continue to meet the pupil's needs. What the auditor should be considering in this scenario is whether the accessible WC is likely to also meet the needs of other disabled people, whether the provision of a single accessible WC is sufficient for the whole school and whether an additional accessible WC facility, equipped in accordance with the provisions of AD M, is required to meet the needs of disabled visitors. Situations such as this require the auditor to keep an open mind and, critically, to enquire about the use of existing facilities from building users. It is rare that any building will follow a precise blueprint and strictly accord with published design guidance – the auditor should make considered judgements in the overall context of the site and / or building and the nature of the service provided.

## 4.5 Making recommendations

In many respects, the recommendations are the most important aspect of an access audit – they provide the client with a clear direction for making decisions and implementing change. In order to be effective, recommendations must be clearly set out, thoroughly explained and sufficiently detailed to enable the client to make decisions and take action.

It is preferable that recommendations are made on the basis of an inclusive design approach that seeks to ensure that everyone can access and benefit from the full range of opportunities available in society.

According to the Centre for Accessible Environments, inclusive design:

• places people at the heart of the design process
• acknowledges human diversity and difference
• offers choice where a single design solution cannot accommodate all users
• provides for flexibility in use
• aims to provide buildings and environments that are convenient, equitable and enjoyable to use by everyone, regardless of ability, age and gender

Inclusive design is an evolving field and subject to continual review and, in some cases, structured research. Design guidance considered today as representing best practice may tomorrow be amended, expanded or superseded. In many cases, design guidance will be expanded as further research and experience is gained in a particular subject area. However, there will be instances, particularly where equipment and safety requirements evolve, where facilities previously considered acceptable in certain circumstances are no longer recommended. An example of this is the provision of platform stairlifts in public buildings, which were permissible in certain circumstances under the provisions of previous editions of AD M, but are no longer considered suitable. Auditors should keep abreast of all such developments to ensure that advice given in audits is up to date.

The key issue for auditors, and one that is often overlooked, is that there is usually more than one way of overcoming a potential barrier to access. There may indeed be several ways of improving access to or usability of a feature or service, including the implementation of permanent physical modifications, temporary physical adjustments, the provision of equipment, changes in management strategy, or changes to the location or the way a service is delivered. Some solutions can offer immediate improvements to the way services are delivered, others provide short-term solutions and some provide permanent improvements, but may take some time to implement. All of these options are relevant.

An important factor likely to influence the range and type of recommendations set out in a report is the timescale for implementation. If the recommendations include the construction of a new ramp and steps to the main entrance of a public building, it is likely to take several months to obtain the necessary planning and building regulations approvals, plus any listed building or landlord consents where relevant. During the process of obtaining consents and at all times up until the ramp and steps are available for use, the service provider still has a duty to make reasonable adjustments to ensure the services in the building are accessible. In the intervening period, this could be achieved in a number of ways, such as providing an alternative accessible entrance, providing a temporary ramp, providing the service in an alternative accessible location or in an alternative way.

This example illustrates that, even where a client does proceed with a permanent physical modification, other solutions for overcoming a physical barrier cannot necessarily be ruled out as they may offer more immediate and short-term alternatives which are key to the availability and accessibility of services.

The factors that influence any decision about what constitutes a 'reasonable adjustment' under equality legislation include the effectiveness and practicality of the change, the extent of disruption, the cost of the work and the resources available, the amount of money already spent on adjustments and the availability of financial or other forms of assistance. It is rare for an auditor to have a comprehensive knowledge of how all these issues affect a client, particularly the issue of available resources. As a result, it is clearly inappropriate for an auditor to make finite recommendations which involve significant expenditure, without also offering alternative solutions that are better suited to clients with potentially fewer resources. This is not an opportunity to get away with providing a less expensive solution, it is a thorough explanation of the alternatives available and should provide sufficient information for the client to make an informed decision on how to proceed.

To what level of detail should recommendations be made? This will depend on a range of factors, including the client's information requirements and particular details of the commission. It is also likely to relate to the client's degree of awareness of access issues and their understanding of relevant legislation. Where recommendations relate to physical modifications, a client's technical knowledge and understanding of the building development processes may influence the required level of detail for the design and dimensional guidance.

For example, the management committee of a community building comprises members representing each of the user groups, none of whom has technical or construction knowledge. Some members have experience of particular impairments, but none has a comprehensive understanding of access or legislative issues. For an audit of the site, building and facilities for this community building to be effective and enable the management committee to make informed decisions, the recommendations will need to clearly explain the options available, why they represent an improvement in accessibility and, where adjustments relate to physical features, give sufficient design and dimensional guidance to fully explain the nature of work. In this scenario, a simple statement such as 'redecorate internal surfaces' is unlikely to be sufficient. The audit should explain the benefits of visual contrast between surfaces and fixtures to people with a visual impairment so that the client is aware of the reason behind the recommendation. It should be clear which elements of the interior should be redecorated to maximise the benefits of visual contrast. Wherever possible, guidance could also be given on sources of further information, as long as these are readily available to the client.

Undertaking an audit of, for example, a local authority premises, commissioned by the estates department in order to identify potential physical improvements prior to a major refurbishment project, is likely to involve a different emphasis when drafting recommendations. As the recipient of the audit report is undoubtedly from a technical background, detailed reproduction of design and dimensional criteria may not always be necessary. Of more relevance is a discussion of any options available for improving access and a consideration of how physical aspects of the building interrelate with operational and management issues.

However recommendations are drafted, it is essential that they are sufficiently detailed and explained to enable the client to make informed decisions and to move on to the next stage in the process of improvements.

## 4.6 Priorities and categories

It is good practice to prioritise and categorise recommendations. From a client's point of view, guidance on the degree of priority for addressing a particular barrier to access is clearly valuable, but from the auditor's point of view, much harder to establish. Priority ratings and categories, where used, should be established in consultation with the client and clearly defined in the audit report.

### Priority ratings

By definition, priorities have an inherent sense of importance and a degree of urgency. Priorities should be attributed to recommendations in the context of the client's circumstances.

A word of caution is required here. Priority ratings are often confused with categories, which can be misleading to the client. For example, priority ratings defined as 'adjustments that can be made immediately', 'work to be undertaken in the next 12 months' and 'major modifications requiring longer term planning' do not necessarily reflect the importance of a particular recommendation. The installation of a passenger lift in an existing multistorey building to which members of the public have access on all floor levels, but which currently has no alternative means of vertical circulation other than the stairs, is likely to be a high priority for the client. However, in the example above, the recommendation to install a lift is likely to fall into the third definition, which is 'major modifications requiring longer term planning'. Being third on the list, the priority rating has, by implication, a reduced sense of importance that is clearly inappropriate for this item of work. The definitions in this example would, in fact, be more appropriately termed categories, as they are classifying work into divisions which simply record how quickly the work could be achieved.

Priority definitions should be established which enable any recommendation to be attributed the appropriate degree of importance, irrespective of the size or nature of the work.

**Priority ratings**

Example 1

1 Items which are likely to significantly improve the accessibility of services and facilities and are strongly recommended for immediate consideration. Also, any item constituting a risk to the health and safety of building users.

2 Additional recommended action to meet best practice guidelines which are likely to improve accessibility for all building users.

Example 2

1 Essential – indicates that the work recommended is essential to provide access which would otherwise be impossible or unsafe.

2 Desirable – indicates that the work recommended is necessary to ensure independent access for some disabled people.

3 Best practice – indicates that the work is required to improve accessibility for all, and ensure that best practice standards are achieved.

## Categories

Categories represent a system of classification which enables audit recommendations to be attributed to various divisions. The divisions may classify the type of improvement, for example redecoration work, building repair or maintenance, a management or policy change or the provision of auxiliary aids and services. Categories may attribute recommendations to particular people or departments in an organisation, for example highways, estates, maintenance, human resources, information technology, and so on. Categories often reflect the structure of the client organisation and their mechanism for implementing recommendations.

**Categories**

Example 1

| | |
|---|---|
| B | Building modification |
| I | Interpretation |
| M | Management |
| H and S | Health and safety |
| T | Staff training |

Example 2

| | |
|---|---|
| M | Management |
| B | Building element (structure and building services) |
| E | Estates (long-term development to be considered) |
| T | Training (staff) |
| O | Other (for example highways) |

Example 3

| | |
|---|---|
| M | Work could be carried out as part of an ongoing maintenance programme |
| R | Indicates that work may be necessary to suit a known individual member of staff |
| O | Indicates that other organisations or authorities may need to provide specialist input or sanction improvements |

## 4.7 Cost banding

Some clients require information on the cost of implementing the recommendations included in an audit report. This is understandable given that a consideration of the cost of an adjustment is likely to have a bearing on any decisions taken on how and when to proceed.

If an auditor has the necessary skills and experience to accurately assess the cost of improvements, there is no reason why cost estimates should not be incorporated into the audit report. The relevant skills are likely to be demonstrated by qualifications in building or quantity surveying, architecture or building management, but current experience is also relevant in order to take account of regional cost variations and other fluctuations in the construction market.

Cost estimates provided within an audit report are likely to be based on an initial inspection of the building only. It is unlikely that detailed investigations will have been made concerning the building fabric or any form of consultation held with a structural engineer. For this reason, any cost advice included in the audit report will be subject to verification following further investigations and should be clearly set out as such.

Given the limitations of providing accurate cost advice at the initial audit stage, it may be preferable to consider the use of cost bands, which provide a useful indication of the likely magnitude of cost for each recommendation. Cost bands can be tailored to suit the range and type of work likely to be required for a particular site or building, and can be as narrow or as broad as a client and auditor consider appropriate.

The provision of cost information in any form can be an effective way of highlighting improvements that can be achieved at no cost. Recommendations in a report should include improvements or changes to, for example, policies, staff attitudes, building management procedures and the method of service delivery, many of which could be implemented with no financial outlay.

The cost band information provides an indication of the estimated cost of each recommendation. This information is provided to help the client prepare budget estimates and future expenditure profiles for implementation of the works. The cost bands represent the net cost of the works and should be regarded as a ball park figure only at this stage. The figures do not include VAT, statutory approval fees or consultant fees.

**Cost bands**

Example 1

| Ref. | Cost band | Example of works |
|------|-----------|------------------|
| 1 | up to £1,000 | Modifications to an accessible WC<br>Supplementary signage |
| 2 | up to £10,000 | New accessible WC<br>Modifications to steps and approaches |
| 3 | £10,000+ | Construction of an external ramp<br>Replacing external stairs |
| 4 | £20,000+ | Installation of new lift / lift shaft |

Example 2

| Cost band | Value of works |
|-----------|----------------|
| A | £0–£500 |
| B | £500–£1,000 |
| C | £1,000–£5,000 |
| D | £5,000–£10,000 |
| E | above £10,000 |

# 5.0 Access audit extracts

This chapter includes extracts based on three completed access audit reports, each relating to a very different type of building – a parish church, the penguin enclosure at London Zoo and a theatre. The extracts have been adapted for the purposes of this publication and are intended to show what an access audit might look like and what type of information may be included.

The parish church audit extract illustrates a tabular report format. This is structured to follow a logical route through the building and clearly record observations of the existing environment alongside recommendations for improvement. The penguin enclosure audit extract is set out in a narrative format, which is more descriptive and good for situations where detailed explanations are useful. The theatre audit extract covers the initial sections of an audit report to illustrate the type of background information and explanatory text that should accompany the detailed audit findings.

None of the examples show the whole original audit report – these are too lengthy for publication. The extracts shown provide a useful example of different report styles and supporting information. In practice, each audit report would include all the sections set out in *Guidelines for audit report structure* (page 45) prior to issue to a client.

# Extract one – Penguin Beach, London Zoo

Penguin Beach is one of the newest exhibits on the London Zoo site and opened in 2011. Penguin Beach provides a new home to two types of penguin: Black-footed Penguins from South Africa and Namibia and Rockhopper Penguins from the sub-Antarctic islands. The new penguin home includes a beach designed to replicate a South American beach landscape and the largest penguin pool in England. The penguins relocated to their new home from the iconic art deco penguin pool designed by Lubetkin.

As well as being designed to provide a suitable living environment for the penguins, Penguin Beach offers facilities for the public, including tiered seating and poolside viewing areas. Regular events are held in the exhibit including the *Penguin Beach Talk* and *Penguin Beach Live!* demonstrations. Daily *Meet the Penguin* encounters take place within the VIP area.

## Exhibit approach

Access into the Penguin Beach exhibit is via a pedestrian path that is gently sloped and has a gradient measured as 1:22. Paths of this gradient should include a level area (or landing) for each 500mm change in level and where there is a change in direction. This is to provide regular rest areas for people who may find it difficult to traverse an inclined surface. There is a drainage gulley set into the path which is not entirely flush with the surface and creates a cross camber. It is suggested that the path levels around the drainage gulley are adjusted as part of the future repair and maintenance programme.

## Penguin viewing areas

The large fish-eye window offers visitors an unusual underwater view of the penguin pool and is an attractive feature in itself, being large enough to enable children to climb into the concave glass. The window is accessed via a short flight of three steps and an adjacent ramp, both of which are well designed and easy to identify. The surface leading immediately up to the viewing window is steeply inclined and has a gradient of 1:5. This is likely to present difficulties to some people who may find it difficult to stand on an inclined surface and for wheelchair users who may risk overbalancing. The requirement for a slight gradient towards the drainage channel is acknowledged here in order to ensure water is drained effectively, but the existing gradient appears excessive. An adjustment to the gradient of the surface immediately in front of the viewing window is recommended to be considered, such as during future maintenance and repairs. As an interim measure, the provision of a grabrail or handle to either side of the viewing window may help some visitors.

Figure 5.1 The fish-eye viewing window provides an unusual underwater view of the penguins, but is approached via a steeply ramped surface which may make it difficult for some people to position themselves close enough to the window to view the underwater environment. The provision of grabrails either side of the window is recommended in the short term, prior to a reduction in the path gradient in the longer term.

The penguin pool has been designed with a glazed perimeter screen to enable the public to view the penguins' underwater environment. The glazed wall has metal support posts at approximately 1200mm centres, which contrast visually with the perimeter path and the water viewed through the screen and thereby serve to highlight the presence of the glass. The change in colour of the glass above and below the waterline also provides an unusual, but nonetheless effective, means of identifying the glass barrier.

Figure 5.2 The glass guarding to the penguin pool forms an effective barrier as well as providing opportunities to view the penguins above and below the waterline. The change in colour above and below the waterline helps to highlight the presence of the glass.

The screen to the perimeter of the penguins' beach environment is also glazed, but supported within a substantial wooden support structure that helps to highlight the presence of the glass while also allowing good visibility into the enclosure for people with different eye levels.

Figure 5.3 The glass guarding to the beach environment enables people at different eye levels to see into the enclosure. The substantial timber base and vertical supports effectively highlight the boundary between the viewing area and enclosure.

## Visitor seating

A tiered seating area is provided to one end of the penguin pool and offers good visibility of the entire enclosure. The tiered seating is heavily used during talks and demonstrations. The steps to the tiered seating are uniform and shallow with step risers measured as 130–140mm high. The step treads are at least 300mm deep and all nosings are highlighted with a contrasting yellow band.

Figure 5.4 The tiered seating provides a viewing area for the *Penguin Beach Live!* demonstrations. The provision of firm handrails is recommended to the steps to provide easier access for all visitors.

Guarding to the tiered seating steps comprises flexible netting mounted between substantial timber posts – there is no firm handrail. The absence of handrails is likely to make it difficult for some people to use the steps, particularly for mobility–impaired people and visually–impaired people. The provision of suitable handrails improves ease of access and safety for everyone.

It is strongly recommended that supplementary fixed handrails be provided to the steps wherever practical, such as in each location where the flexible netting is installed. Handrails are recommended to be tubular (32–50mm diameter) or oval (50mm x 39mm overall dimensions) in profile and should be firmly fixed at a height of 900–1000mm above the pitch line of the steps and 1000–1100mm above landings. Handrails should contrast visually with the surrounding surfaces so that they are easy to identify and should be of a material that is not cold to touch. A timber handrail is likely to be suitable in this environment and be in keeping with the style and materials of the existing step supports and guarding. The handrails should be mounted on brackets that provide at least 50mm clearance between the mounting posts (or wall) and the handrail. This clearance is to ensure a person does not have to lift their hand off the rail while ascending or descending a flight of steps.

At the poolside level of the tiered seating there are a number of designated spaces for wheelchair users and these are clearly marked with the International Symbol for Access. There is a slight gradient to the surface in this area which will ensure effective drainage of surface water. At the time of the audit the designated spaces were being used as overflow pushchair storage areas, but staff noted that this is closely monitored and only permitted when there are no wheelchair users requiring access.

**Viewing platform**
The raised viewing platform in front of the Base Camp hut offers an alternative vantage point to view the penguin pool and is accessed via a short flight of steps and a ramp. The steps are similar in configuration to the tiered seating steps and have no firm handrail above the mesh guarding. It is recommended that handrails are provided to both sides of the steps in accordance with the design guidance set out above.

The ramp comprises a lower and upper flight, separated by a large intermediate landing. The ramp slopes appear to be slightly uneven and have a gradient measured in places as 1:9, noted to be significantly steeper than the maximum permissible gradient of 1:12 set out in the provisions of Approved Document M (AD M). The lower ramp slope has no handrails, whereas the upper ramp slope has tubular handrails to both sides, fixed at a height of 900–1000mm above the ramp surface.

Figure 5.5 The ramp to the raised viewing platform requires handrails to the lower slope to match those already provided to the upper slope.

It is recommended that the existing ramp be reviewed in detail to ascertain whether the overall rise and ramp length meet the provisions of AD M. If so, it is likely that regrading of the ramp surface will be sufficient to provide an even and gently sloping surface that will facilitate safe and easy access for wheelchair users. If it is found that the average gradient and length of the existing ramp slopes exceed the provisions of AD M, the recommendation would be for reconstruction of the ramp.

In the short term, it is recommended that handrails be provided to both sides of the lower ramp slope. If practical, the handrail should be continuous around the intermediate landing. It would be appropriate to provide a similar style handrail to those already installed to the upper ramp slope.

**Directional signage**
There is minimal directional signage within the Penguin Beach exhibit, and none high-lighting the location of the designated wheelchair seating area or the ramp to the raised viewing platform. While both of these facilities may be obvious when the exhibit is quiet, at busy times they are often obscured from view.

It is recommended that the location of the designated wheelchair seating area and ramp are clearly identified on maps of the exhibit and on directional signage within the Penguin Beach enclosure. Suitable management policies should also be established to ensure that staff are able to guide or accompany people through the crowd at busy times to the designated seating area or viewing platform, if the need arises.

# Extract two – Almeida Theatre

The following is an extract from the report of an access audit of the Almeida Theatre in London. The extract is of the initial sections of a large audit report and provides an example of how relevant background and supporting information may be set out. The summary and tabular section, which records detailed observations and recommendations for improvements, are not included in this extract, but would logically follow in sections 2.0 and 3.0, as noted in the sample contents list below.

**Contents page** *(include page numbers when producing your report to assist readers)*

## 1.0 Introduction

### 1.1 Client brief and scope of audit

This access audit report has been produced for the Almeida Theatre, Islington. The report records the findings and recommendations arising from an access audit of the theatre building and immediate surroundings. The access audit covers all public areas of the building as well as access for performers and staff.

The audit is an assessment of the accessibility and usability of the building and immediate surroundings for disabled people. However, it should be noted that the issues considered in the report affect the convenience of access to and use of the building for all its occupants, not just those with identifiable impairments. The approach advocated is based on inclusive design principles, which aim to improve the usability of the building and services for all users regardless of age, ability or gender.

The report records and assesses the current situation with regard to specific physical elements of the building and site, as well as management procedures and staff awareness and training. Potential barriers to access are noted in the report alongside recommendations to improve access and usability.

### 1.2 Description of building

The Almeida Theatre is in Islington and is a thriving venue for British and international drama. The theatre building comprises a Grade II listed building accommodating the auditorium and backstage areas and a modern foyer and bar. The theatre reopened in 2003 after a two-year major refurbishment that incorporated a large number of access improvements to the site.

The auditorium holds 325 seats over two levels, stalls and circle. The circle, which has approximately 115 seats, has stepped access only. A minimum of two or three spaces are allocated to wheelchair users in the stalls in each performance. Additional spaces can be provided when the need arises by altering the layout of the first three rows of seats in the stalls.

The box office is located in the foyer and is open to the public Monday to Saturday from 10am until 6pm and for collection of tickets before evening performances until 7:30pm. Bookings can be made online or by telephone.

The café / bar is open to the public throughout the day, Monday to Saturday, from 11:30am until 11pm.

The theatre website includes a very helpful section under the headings 'Access' and 'Facilities', which illustrates and describes features of the building such as the main entrance, the availability of steps and ramps, toilet provision, counter provision within the café / bar and auditorium facilities.

The theatre timetable includes a number of assisted performances, including stage text-captioned performances, audio-described performances and BSL-interpreted performances. An infrared hearing enhancement system is available in the main auditorium, with headsets available to borrow from the foyer kiosk. An induction loop is available at the box office counter.

All the theatre staff consulted before and during the audit survey appeared to be very knowledgeable about access issues and all were observed to be extremely helpful to visitors and performers on site at the time.

## 1.3   Criteria for assessment

The criteria for assessment are as follows:
- The need to maximise access into and throughout the building, in terms of facilities for members of the public, performance and staff
- The provisions in Approved Document Part M of the Building Regulations, 2004 edition
- Current guidance on the provisions of the Equality Act 2010
- The need to observe reasonable practical and financial implications of implementing recommendations to improve access
- Guidance in BS 8300:2009 *Design of buildings and their approaches to meet the needs of disabled people. Code of practice.* British Standards Institution, 2009
- Guidance in BS 9999:2008 *Code of practice for fire safety in the design, management and use of buildings.* British Standards Institution, 2008
- Guidance in BS EN 81-70:2003 *Safety rules construction and installation. Particular applications for passenger and goods passenger lifts. Accessibility to lifts for persons including persons with disability.* British Standards Institution, 2003
- Currently published good practice in design and detailing which meets the needs of disabled people, including:
  - *Manual for Streets*, Department for Transport, 2007
  - *Designing for Accessibility*, CAE / RIBA Publications, 2012
  - Personal Emergency Egress Plans, Northern Officers Group, 1993
  - *Sign Design Guide – A guide to inclusive signage*, P Barker and J Fraser, Mobility Unit and the Sign Design Society, 2004
  - *SLL Code for Lighting* (Society of Light and Lighting). Chartered Institute of Building Services Engineers (CIBSE), 2012

- Specifiers' Handbooks for Inclusive Design:
  *Architectural Ironmongery*
  *Automatic Door Systems*
  *Internal Floor Finishes*
  *Glass in Buildings*
  *Platform Lifts*
  CAE / RIBA Publications, 2005 and 2006

- Dimensional criteria used in the report based on the guidance given in Approved Document Part M, 2004 edition and BS 8300:2009.

## 1.4 Legislative context

In October 2010, the Disability Discrimination Acts 1995 and 2005 (DDA) were superseded by the Equality Act 2010. The Equality Act (the Act) aims to unify different pieces of equality legislation to provide greater consistency and, in some areas, to strengthen provisions. The Act is structured around nine different 'protected characteristics', one of which is disability. It aims to prohibit discrimination, harassment and victimisation. Under the Act there is a duty at large to reasonably predict and cater for the needs of disabled people as well as a vicarious liability in respect of the actions of members of staff.

The Act defines a disabled person as 'someone who has a physical or mental impairment, which has a substantial and long-term adverse effect on his or her ability to carry out normal day-to-day activities', where 'substantial' is defined as 'more than minor or trivial'. Compared to the DDA, it should now be easier for disabled people to show they meet the definition of disability. Government figures indicate that over 10 million disabled adults in the UK and approximately 700,000 disabled children are covered by this legislation.

Under the Act, discrimination now includes:
- direct discrimination, where, because of their disability, a disabled person receives worse treatment than somebody who does not have that disability
- indirect discrimination, where a policy, rule or practice which is applied to everyone places people with a particular disability at a disadvantage compared with people who do not have that disability, unless it can be justified
- discrimination arising from disability, where a disabled person is treated unfavourably not because of the disability itself but because of something connected with their disability, unless it can be justified

The Equality Act also places duties on providers of goods, facilities and services (Part 3), employers (Part 5), those leasing or selling land or property (Part 4) and education providers (Part 6). While the Act does not directly require accessible environments to be provided for disabled people, it requires that, where disabled people are placed at a 'substantial disadvantage', 'reasonable adjustments' be made to avoid the disadvantage caused by policies and practices or physical features, and to provide auxiliary aids.

The Act does not override other legislation relating to buildings such as planning, building regulations, listed building and fire regulations. The Act itself does not include guidance on the design of buildings; in this regard, it is advisable to follow current best practice design guidance as referred to in this report in order to be able to justify any decisions taken in relation to the implementation of reasonable adjustments.

The duty to make reasonable adjustments occurs where disabled people experience a 'substantial disadvantage' in fulfilling their roles at work, or in accessing goods and services for example. This is in contrast to the DDA, where service providers were only required to make adjustments if it was 'impossible or unreasonably difficult' for disabled people to access their services. The requirements of the duty reflect the DDA duties but in a more consistent way.

Under the Act, service providers should consider making adjustments to:

- provisions, criteria and practices that govern the way in which goods, services and facilities are made accessible to disabled people
- physical features by removing or altering a physical feature (or by providing a reasonable means of avoiding it), or providing a reasonable alternative method of making the services available to disabled people
- the provision of auxiliary aids and services to make it easier for disabled people to make use of and access goods, facilities or services

Further information on the Equality Act 2010 can be obtained from the Equality and Human Rights Commission's website at www.equalityhumanrights.com

### 1.5 Disclaimer

This report has been prepared by reference to a view of current best practice that is subject to change.

As the Equality Act 2010 is not compliance based, adherence to the advice contained in this report cannot ensure compliance with the Equality Act or immunity from the award of damages under the Act.

For information regarding any issues arising from the interpretation of the Equality Act, it is strongly recommended that you seek appropriate legal advice.

## 1.6 Factors contributing to accessibility

There are many factors contributing to accessibility, the most obvious being the building's shell. However, it is also important to consider fixtures and fittings, furniture and equipment.

As well as this, it is vital to consider how a building is or will be used. How a building is managed during its day-to-day operation will have a significant impact on how easily disabled people can use the building. The awareness and attitudes of staff and volunteers will have a fundamental impact on how people use the building, and will help to determine whether it is safe and convenient to use. For these reasons, in addition to physical aspects of the building, the access audit will consider the role of management, as well as staffing and staff training. For more information on building management issues, refer to the Building management section of *Designing for Accessibility*.

## 1.8 Audit details

• Auditor name(s)
• Meetings with client representatives and others
• Date(s) of audit survey

The audit of the Almeida Theatre was conducted on a bright clear day.

• Drawings / information available:
  Printed theatre programme
  A4 outline theatre plans

## 1.9 Glossary of abbreviations

The following abbreviations are used throughout the report.

| | |
|---|---|
| AD M | Approved Document M of the building regulations (2004 edition - incorporating 2010 and 2013 amendments) |
| BS 8300 | BS 8300:2009 Design of buildings and their approaches to meet the needs of disabled people. Code of Practice |
| ecw | effective clear width (measured from the face of the door when open to the opposite frame or doorstop, taking into account the door handle or any other door furniture) |
| ffl | finished floor level |

## 1.10 Report format

A summary of the results of the audit and the key recommendations are set out in section 2.0 of this report. The detailed results of the audit are set out in the tables in section 3.0, using the following format:

**Column 1**    Reference number
**Column 2**    Specific location / element name
**Column 3**    Brief description of or comment on the existing situation
**Column 4**    Recommendations for improvement, including relevant references
**Column 5**    Priority or category reference

## 1.11 Explanation of priority ratings and classifications

**P1**    Public area – high priority
**P2**    Public area – medium priority
**P3**    Public area – at next major refurbishment

**S1**    Staff area – minor alteration
**S2**    Staff area – medium priority, alter if staff requires, or at next refurbishment
**S3**    Staff area – major alteration required

**Mnt**    Maintenance issue
**Mgt**    Management issue

Figure 5.6 The Almeida Theatre is distinctive within the streetscape and comprises a Grade II listed building and modern addition. The large glazed doors have a level threshold and provide direct access to the foyer and box office.

Figure 5.7 The ramp and adjacent steps bridge the change in level between the entrance foyer and historic auditorium and also provide direct access to male, female and unisex accessible toilet facilities. The ramp has kerb edgings to both sides and handrails to the full length of the ramp slopes on both sides.

Figure 5.8 The male and female toilet areas each include a larger cubicle with an outward-opening door and fixed grabrails to either side of the WC. Signage on the outside of the cubicle door usefully states 'wide cubicle with handrail'.

Figure 5.9 Careful detailing of contemporary handrails and the selection of visually contrasting colours demonstrates good practice in terms of accessibility while also preserving historical elements of the original theatre building.

# Extract three – St John's Church, Notting Hill

St John's church is understood to have been constructed around 1850. The current church is largely the same as the original in terms of overall layout, although some changes have been made internally to the worship and meeting areas in recent years. The altar has recently been repositioned within the nave and a quiet area for worship has been created in the chancel. A meeting room links the main church with the tower. An office and meeting room are located at first floor level, but access to these is restricted to church officials only. The tower stair is the original stair and is not considered suitable for public access in its current form. Two small toilets have been installed below the stair.

A programme of repair, refurbishment and alterations is proposed to care for the existing building fabric and to make the church suitable for wider community use. Structural repairs to the tower have just been completed and further work to safeguard the building fabric is planned, for which funding has already been secured. Other planned work includes removal of the organ, replacement of lighting within the nave and meeting room and replacement of the existing timber pews with moveable chairs.

In addition to church services, the building is used by a number of other groups for meetings and events. These include a parent and toddler group, Boy Scouts and Girl Guides. The church facilities have also been used for parties, fashion shows and for musical events.

Figure 5.10 The existing timber pews are positioned in a traditional arrangement either side of the central aisle. The pews are proposed to be replaced with individual moveable chairs which can be arranged to suit different events and services. The new arrangement is likely to be much more inclusive.

Figure 5.11 The altar is currently on a raised platform accessed via three steps. The proposed changes to the seating arrangement and altar position will offer level access to all parts of the worship area.

Figure 5.12 When the floor finishes are renewed, the opportunity should be taken to provide contrasting step nosings to the altar platform. The provision of sensitively designed handrails should also be considered – they could be positioned close to the columns on each side of the steps.

## 3.0 Worship areas

| Ref | Item and photo | Current situation | Recommendations |
| --- | --- | --- | --- |
| 3.1 | **Seating**<br><br>(Refer to Figure 5.10) | The congregation area is currently fitted with fixed timber pews in a traditional arrangement either side of a central aisle. The pews are all proposed to be removed and replaced in the near future with individual moveable chairs which can be positioned in different arrangements for services and events. The new chairs will provide flexibility in the seating layout and give a wide choice of seating position for wheelchair users. | The proposed new seating arrangement is considered to be inherently accessible and will provide the flexibility to meet individual needs in an inclusive manner. |
| 3.2 | **Seat style** | The proposed new seats to the congregation area are to be timber framed with padded seats and backrests. At this stage, no seats with armrests are proposed. | It is recommended that a number of chairs with armrests are also provided, plus a small number of chairs with a high back. Armrests greatly benefit people with reduced strength and impaired mobility as they provide support to people when raising and lowering themselves in the chair. Providing a wider range of chairs will cater for a broader range of needs within the existing and future congregation. |

| Ref | Item and photo | Current situation | Recommendations |
|-----|----------------|-------------------|-----------------|
| 3.3 | **Floor** | The existing floor in the pew areas is timber boarded and painted black. The boards are old and undulating. When the timber pews are removed, it is understood that the timber boards are to be replaced with new hardwood flooring to provide a smooth, level floor.<br><br>The existing pink aisle carpet is currently firmly fixed along all edges with a slimline edge trim – this is a good feature. The carpet is proposed to be removed when the seats are removed. | The proposed modifications to the floor finishes are considered suitable. Junctions between different floor materials are recommended to be flush with minimal gaps in any joints.<br><br>Removal of the carpet may affect the acoustic characteristics of the church as there will be more 'harder' surfaces, which reflect rather than absorb sound. This may be balanced to some degree by the introduction of the upholstered seats. The situation should be monitored once the changes have been made. |
| 3.4 | **Altar platform**<br><br>(Refer to Figure 5.11) | The altar is currently positioned on a large raised platform at the east end of the nave. The platform is also used by groups of musicians and is currently the main focus for the delivery of church services. This is likely to change when the seating arrangement is altered as there will be greater potential to conduct services from the main floor level, with a variety of chair and altar arrangements. Reverend (Rev) Stephenson noted that a new altar table is proposed which will be moveable and can be used either on the raised platform or at the main floor level of the church. | The potential to deliver services in a range of formats and in different areas of the church is a significant development. This will enable services to be tailored to meet individual and group needs. Notwithstanding this, consideration should still be given to the provision of a ramp to the existing altar platform to enable access by wheelchair users. It is acknowledged that a ramp will be lengthy and may prove to be unfeasible. However, potential options should be explored to investigate the feasibility of a new ramp and whether this could be designed to complement the proposed new seating arrangements. |

| Ref | Item and photo | Current situation | Recommendations |
|---|---|---|---|
| 3.5 | **Altar steps**<br><br>(Refer to Figure 5.12) | Access to the existing altar platform is via three steps with varying tread and riser dimensions. It is understood that the varying depth treads allow for communion to be served to people kneeling on the lowest step. The deeper second step provides space for church officials. The steps and upper altar floor area are fully carpeted with a plain pink carpet. There is no visually contrasting nosing to the leading edge of the steps.<br><br>There are no handrails to the altar steps. | When the floor finishes are renewed as part of the planned refurbishment and renewal works, it is recommended that the opportunity be taken to improve visual contrast between the steps and altar platform and to effectively highlight each step edge. Step nosings should be firm and non-slip, but in the case of the altar step, the selection of surface finishes should take account of the fact that people will, on occasion, continue to kneel in this location in order to receive communion.<br><br>It is recommended that permanent handrails be provided to either side of the altar platform, such as fixed on or adjacent to the stone pillars. The handrails will need to be sensitively designed to reflect the architectural style of the church, but should meet current guidelines for height, length and visual contrast. |
| 3.6 | **Communion rail** | Two moveable benches are used to form a communion rail and are positioned on the lowest altar step. There is no fixed communion rail. | The use of moveable benches as a communion rail is supported as it provides the opportunity to use the rail in other areas, such as at the main floor level. Again, flexibility in how services can be delivered provides the best opportunity for an inclusive environment. |

| Ref | Item and photo | Current situation | Recommendations |
|---|---|---|---|
| 3.7 | **Pulpit** | A raised pulpit is located to the north side of the altar platform. Rev Stephenson noted that it is useful to be able to preach from a raised area when the church is full, but otherwise preaching can be undertaken from any other position in the church.<br><br>It is understood that a new, moveable and height-adjustable lectern is to be purchased in the near future. This will support the flexible arrangements of how services are delivered. | No recommendations are made other than for flexibility to be maintained in the way services are conducted. |
| 3.8 | **Service format** | Rev Stephenson noted that part of the preparation for services such as weddings and funerals is to discuss individual need with the family and if access requirements are identified, these are taken into account in the way the service is arranged. In discussions, it was apparent that Rev Stephenson and other members of the congregation have a high level of awareness of access issues and are sensitive to individual and wider needs within the community. There appears to be an ongoing review of how best to deliver inclusive and accessible services and facilities. | The current approach to the delivery of services is fully supported. As physical improvements are made to the building, an ongoing review of arrangements will need to be made and developed in conjunction with the congregation. |

| Ref | Item and photo | Current situation | Recommendations |
|---|---|---|---|
| 3.9 | **Order of service papers** | Printed leaflets are prepared each week for scheduled church services. Large print versions are currently prepared for individuals within the congregation. There is no current requirement by any existing member of the congregation for Braille or audio-described information. | It is suggested that a local Braille transcription service be identified so that documents can be prepared promptly in the future if required by a member of the congregation. Similarly, identification of an individual or organisation able to produce audio-described material locally may also be useful. |
| 3.10 | **Lighting** | The existing artificial lights throughout the church, but particularly to the congregation area, comprise pendant fittings. The quality and distribution of light is considered to be poor. | The light fittings are recommended to be replaced with new fittings that provide increased level of illuminance throughout the church. The design and selection of fittings should ensure that lighting levels are even, provide good colour rendition and are easy to control. Light fittings should not be positioned where they are likely to cause glare, shadows or silhouettes. |
| 3.11 | **Public address / sound system** | A music system is currently installed in the church, with two large speakers mounted on the east wall of the main congregation area. Rev Stephenson is currently considering installing supplementary speakers for the north and south walls to improve the quality of spoken word through the system and is obtaining specialist technical advice on this issue. | The proposed improvements to the existing sound system are supported and should benefit all building users, but particularly people with hearing impairments. |

| Ref | Item and photo | Current situation | Recommendations |
|---|---|---|---|
| | | Rev Stephenson is clearly very knowledgeable on the operation and performance of sound systems and seeks to ensure that the existing system is used effectively. He also obtains regular feedback from members of the congregation and is currently establishing guidelines for all the people who operate the system to ensure that sound levels are adequate and consistent.<br><br>A radio microphone is used for smaller services conducted on the raised altar platform as sound can be picked up by hearing aid users and it is a preferable arrangement to using the central PA system. | It is excellent practice to regularly seek feedback from members of the congregation and to ensure that anyone who operates the system is fully trained and able to use the equipment effectively. |
| 3.12 | **Permanent induction loop** | A permanent induction loop is installed to the whole of the main church (worship area) and is regularly used by some members of the congregation.<br><br>There was no sign visible in the church highlighting the fact that an induction loop is available. | Wherever induction loops are installed, they should be clearly signed with the appropriate standard public information symbol. A symbol sign is recommended to be situated close to the main entrance doors and on or adjacent to the internal doors into the church, so that people entering the worship area are made aware of the presence of the equipment. |

| Ref | Item and photo | Current situation | Recommendations |
|---|---|---|---|
| 3.13 | **Portable induction loop** | There are currently no portable induction loops in the church. | It is recommended that at least one portable induction loop be provided for use in the ground floor meeting rooms.<br><br>Once a portable induction loop is available, a sign should be provided to indicate that the equipment is available. The equipment should also be tested regularly and training given to anyone responsible for organising events, meetings or activities in the church. |

# 6.0 Case study

## Case study – Hebden Bridge Town Hall

The redevelopment of Hebden Bridge Town Hall and the creation of a new business enterprise centre, the Creative Quarter, is a flagship project in the centre of Hebden Bridge that admirably demonstrates how an existing building can be made more accessible, not only in physical terms, but in a socially inclusive and democratic way. At the heart of the redevelopment process has been an overriding commitment to inclusive design and to effective engagement with the local community.

Hebden Bridge Town Hall

### Building history

Hebden Bridge is a thriving former mill town nestled in the South Pennines, which grew in size and prominence during the nineteenth century, primarily through the development of water-powered weaving mills, clothing manufacture and the advent of the Leeds to Manchester railway. Much of the current town centre was developed during the 1880s and 1890s when the town's population quickly expanded.

Hebden Bridge Town Hall was constructed during this period of rapid expansion and was completed in 1897. An adjoining fire station was added soon after in a matching style and in 1901 a transmission station was constructed to the rear to power the tram service between Hebden Bridge and Halifax. The transmission station was converted into the town library in 1917 and later into additional office accommodation linked to the Town Hall, then finally into community facilities. The original Town Hall is a Grade II listed building.

Latterly, although the Town Hall and adjoining former fire station remained a significant landmark within the town, it had been poorly maintained for many years, was under-used and largely inaccessible. The Town Hall had a stepped main entrance and multiple internal level changes. Ramped access was available into the lower floor of the community rooms to the rear, but there was no alternative means of access to the first floor council chamber, meeting rooms and office accommodation.

**Asset transfer**

The summer of 2006 marked the start of a process that has successfully transformed the existing Town Hall into a thriving community enterprise hub, used by, managed and controlled by the local community. From the start, the process was open to all and driven by a very broad and democratic group committed to social inclusion and which regularly sought the views and input of the wider community. A charitable trust, the Hebden Bridge Community Association Limited (the Association), was formed in 2008 and is now the body responsible for the building and its ongoing operation.

Membership of the Association is open to individuals and organisations and exceeds 600 just a few months after opening. Democracy and accountability to the local community are central to the ethos of the Association and to the project as a whole.

The original Town Hall and adjacent land was transferred to the Association in April 2010 under Calderdale Council's Framework Policy for Community Management of Assets, which had been adopted by the authority the previous year. Hebden Bridge is one of the first communities in the UK to own and manage its own Town Hall, which it now holds under a 125-year leasehold ownership.

Following the asset transfer, the Association pursued funding for major capital redevelopment for the land surrounding the Town Hall – this held the key to making the existing building accessible and to providing additional complementary facilities. The Association's mission for the development of community and enterprise facilities for the town included:

• To maximise use of the building for community and civic purposes
• To secure the future of the building in terms of the economic, community and civic life of the town
• To be socially inclusive, accessible and vibrant
• To be a welcoming building with open space at its centre
• To promote sustainable economic development within the local area
• To be an innovative community-led project at the heart of Hebden Bridge

**Process and consultation**

An access audit of the existing Town Hall was undertaken in 2004 by the local authority. This highlighted a number of barriers to disabled people, including the stepped main entrance, multiple internal changes in level and the absence of any lift or other alternative permanent means of access to the upper floors, in particular the council chamber. The height of the reception counter, door opening widths, sanitary facilities, internal lighting levels and decorations were all noted to fall below the design standards at the time, and there was no hearing enhancement system in the council chamber or elsewhere in the building.

The Association's project brief for the redevelopment proposals included an overriding commitment to inclusive design. The Association formed an access panel to advise and inform the project team and their input proved invaluable as the project progressed. The panel included a number of local disabled people as well as the Chair of the Disability Partnership, Calderdale Council's Disability Liaison Officer and Access Officer, and representatives from Hebden Royd Town Council.

Jade Smith, a councillor at the time and also a wheelchair user, was consulted during the early design stages and was able to give the design team a personal account of the difficulties in accessing the first floor council chamber as well as suggestions for potential improvements. Jade regularly accessed the council chamber using a powered stair-climbing device, operated by one of a number of staff who had received specific training in using the equipment. Although this device provided Jade with an alternative means of access in the short term, it was obvious that a longer-term solution that offered independent access to all building users was needed. Powered stair-climbers are widely acknowledged to be somewhat undignified and can be frightening for the user.

The project architect was Bauman Lyons Architects, an award-winning Leeds-based practice. An access consultant was appointed to the design team and played a key role in ensuring accessibility was considered to all areas of the building from the concept design stages through to project completion. The access consultant produced a detailed access statement to accompany the planning application, which recorded the strategic and detailed design decisions taken by the project team.

**Result**

The Association successfully secured a £1.2 million grant from the European Regional Development Fund and a £2 million loan and grant package from the social investment business *Community builders*. Construction began in April 2011 and was completed in August 2012, and the building brought immediately into use.

Hebden Bridge Creative Quarter forms part of the redevelopment complex and comprises workspace for around 30 small businesses, plus a business lounge and meeting rooms for businesses predominantly from the creative, digital and media sectors.

The completed building includes:

- A purpose-built public hall and function room with a capacity of 200 people and suitable for meetings, conferences, events, performances, weddings and civil partnerships, and parties
- A suite of meeting rooms of different sizes
- Hebden Bridge Creative Quarter: enterprise units for small businesses
- Catering facilities
- Riverside courtyard

A few months after completion, the building is thriving in all respects. Regular diverse events have been held in the Waterfront Hall, including conferences, theatrical performances, craft fairs and social events. The enterprise units are virtually all occupied and the café is a popular meeting place. The local authority's Customer First Service Centre is located centrally on the ground floor of the building and is easily accessed by staff and customers.
Significantly, the original Town Hall building has now been made accessible. All existing internal floor levels can be accessed via a lift or platform lift and independent access is now possible to the main council chamber, which has been retained in its original form.

On an individual level, the success of the redevelopment is demonstrated by the photographs in this case study, which have all been taken by amateur photographer and former Councillor Jade Smith, who is now able to access independently and with dignity the whole of the Hebden Bridge Town Hall, including the original building and council chamber.

Figure 6.1: The main entrance to the existing Town Hall was accessed via a flight of steps.

Figure 6.2: The design of the bespoke reception desk is welcoming and provides access on both sides for wheelchair users. The plywood layers forming the front of the desk are individually profiled to form a tactile map of the Calder Valley and are illuminated through a translucent panel.

Figure 6.3: The difference in ground floor level between the original Town Hall and new extension is bridged with a short flight of steps (above left) and a short-rise platform lift (above right). The steps have contrasting nosings and handrails to each side and are clearly visible from the new main entrance foyer.

Figure 6.4: The short-rise platform lift has a clear landing at the lower and upper levels, which are set back from the main circulation routes. The platform lift controls are post-mounted and clearly visible on approach to the lift.

Figures 6.5 and 6.6: This glazed corridor (pictured internally, left, and externally, right) links the entrance foyers of the original Town Hall and new extension. It provides a spacious and attractive circulation route as well as a vantage point for viewing the riverside courtyard.

Figure 6.7: The new extension provides level internal access from the Waterfront Hall to the riverside courtyard and balcony.

Figure 6.8: The ground floor unisex accessible toilet demonstrates effective visual contrast between floor and wall surfaces, sanitaryware and fixtures. The addition of a padded backrest to the WC would be beneficial.

Figures 6.9 and 6.10: The Creative Quarter entrance is raised above footpath level and accessed via a linear ramp (below) and short flight of steps (below right). Both are shielded from the weather by being set back from the principal elevation of the building. The cedar wall cladding provides effective visual contrast with the surface of the stone steps and ramp and with the stainless steel handrails.

Figure 6.11: Poignant words from poet and author John Siddique are here applied to the full-height glazed entrance screen and form unique but effective markings to highlight the presence of glass.

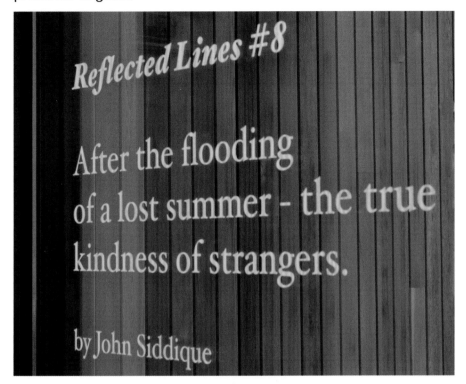

Figure 6.12: This ground floor emergency exit route from the staff office slopes gradually to meet the level of the adjoining footpath.

# 7.0 Access audit checklists

The checklists on the following pages each cover one element of a building or its setting. The checklists broadly follow the order and correspond to the headings in the CAE / RIBA Publishing design guide, Designing for Accessibility (2012 edition). This is an up-to-date and user-friendly good practice guide based on Approved Document M (2004 edition) and BS 8300:2009.

The checklists are also available in Word document and PDF format from CAE. The checklists can be printed or photocopied for use on site, so that the pack can be used to audit a complex building or to audit any number of buildings. Individual checklists can be reproduced several times to record multiple elements of a particular feature, where necessary. For example, several copies of checklist 15 Seating may be required in a building with several different seating areas, particularly if each area differs significantly.

The checklists are intended as aide-memoires and may provide a useful way of carrying out as thorough an audit as possible. They also provide comprehensive source material for writing up an access audit report and / or talking through key recommendations with a client. Completed checklists do not in themselves constitute an access audit report.

## Access audit checklists

### External environment
1   Car parking
2   Setting-down points
3   Pedestrian routes
4   Shared spaces
5   Street furniture
6   External ramps
7   External steps
8   Handrails

### Internal environment
9   Entrances
10  Doors – external and internal
11  Doors – access control systems
12  Doors – opening and closing systems
13  Entrance foyers
14  Reception desks and service counters
15  Seating
16  Horizontal circulation
17  Surfaces

18  Internal ramps, steps and stairs
19  Passenger lifts
20  Platform lifts
21  Sanitary facilities
22  Wayfinding, information and signs
23  Communication systems and acoustics
24  Switches and controls
25  Lighting

**Building management**
26  Building management checklist

**Communications**
27      Information
        Clear print
        Large print
        Braille
        Telephone services
        Audio tape
        Digital
28  Websites
29  Communication services

# Car parking 1

## General provision

**1.1** Is there designated parking provision for disabled motorists?

**1.2** Is the proportion of designated bays compared to standard bays sufficient?

**1.3** Are there any enlarged standard spaces to allow for future expansion?

**1.4** Is there an additional large designated bay for commercial vehicles with integral hoists?

**1.5** Are the designated bays clearly signposted from car park entrance?

- Identified as provision for disabled drivers or passengers only?
- Clearly signposted at each change in direction or change in level?

## Location and arrangement

**1.6** Are the designated bays close to the building entrance?

- If not, is the route to the entrance covered, with seating provided at intervals?

**1.7** In multistorey car parks, are the designated bays at the same level as the principal entrance and exit level?

- If not, is a lift or ramp provided?
- Are the bays grouped together and in the same location at each floor level?

**1.8** Are bays adequately sized?

**1.9** Can car doors be fully opened to allow disabled drivers and passengers to transfer to a wheelchair parked alongside?

**1.10** Is there sufficient space for tail loading?

**1.11** Are designated bays level, smooth, even and free from loose stones?

**1.12** Are designated bays clearly highlighted with a ground-painted symbol and wall- or post-mounted sign?

**1.13** Are the routes from the parking area to ticket machines and buildings accessible, with dropped kerbs and appropriate tactile warnings?

  • Are the routes positioned away from the rear of vehicles?

**1.14** Are routes adequately lit?

## Barriers, control systems and ticket machines

**1.15** Do height barriers provide adequate clearance?

  • Is the clearance consistent throughout the car park?

  • Is there adequate warning of height restrictions and signposting to alternative designated parking spaces?

**1.16** Are access-control systems accessible to all users?

**1.17** Is information about car parking charges clearly displayed?

  • Is it clear if free parking is available to disabled motorists?

**1.18** Can ticket dispensing machines at the car park entrance be used by all motorists without leaving their vehicles?

**1.19** Are ticket dispensing and payment machines accessible?

  • Controls and coin slots at a suitable height?

  • Clear unobstructed kerb-free approach?

## On-street parking

**1.20**   Does the bay arrangement enable safe access
via both sides and the rear of a vehicle?

- Is the bay adequately sized?

**1.21**   Is there kerb-free access to one end of the
bay?

**1.22**   Is the bay on level ground?

**1.23**   Are bay markings and signposting clear?

General observations:

# Setting-down points   **2**

**2.1**   Is a setting-down point provided at a convenient point?

- Clearly signposted?
- Located on level ground?
- Protected from the weather?

**2.2**   Is a separate setting down / waiting area provided for taxis and dial-a-ride vehicles?

**2.3**   Clearly signed to and from the site entrance?

**2.4**   Located as close as possible to the principal entrance (or alternative accessible entrance)?

**2.5**   Sufficiently sized to enable transfer from side door and for tail loading?

**2.6**   Level access provided between the vehicular carriageway and footway?

**2.7**   Area with raised kerb for people transferring into and out of vehicles with fold-out ramps?

General observations:

# Pedestrian routes

**3**

## Layout and gradients

**3.1**   Are access routes from the edge of the site to the principal entrance (or alternative accessible entrance), or from the designated parking area to the entrance, or to other main routes on site, level or near level?

**3.2**   Are passing places provided at junctions and corners of access routes and at regular intervals?

- Are they large enough for people to pass each other?

**3.3**   Is seating provided at regular intervals?

- Set back from the access route?
- Clear space to both sides of fixed seating?

**3.4**   Are routes sufficiently wide?

**3.5**   Is there adequate clear headroom to the full length of the access route?

**3.6**   Where gradients between 1:60 and 1:20 are unavoidable, are level landings provided at intervals?

**3.7**   Where gradients are greater than 1:20, are ramps provided?
(See checklist 6 External ramps)

**3.8**   Do paths have a suitable crossfall gradient?

**3.9**   Signage and landmarks to aid orientation?

**3.10**   Planting used to identify routes or hazards?

- Kept well trimmed?

## Surfaces and drainage

**3.11**   Are surfaces firm, durable, smooth and slip - resistant in all weather conditions?

- Are they well maintained?
- Do different adjacent materials have similar frictional characteristics?
- Have minimal deviations in level?
- Suitable edges?

**3.12**   Are sound qualities, textures and colours of surfaces used to highlight routes?

**3.13**   Are drainage channels and gratings set outside of the access route?

- Are they flush with the paving surface?
- Are the slots and grating openings small enough to avoid presenting a trip hazard?

## Signage and lighting

**3.14**   Are signs suitably located?

- Easy to see, clear and logical?

**3.15**   Are routes and potential hazards adequately lit?

**3.16**   Are lights positioned to provide an even level of illumination and to avoid glare?

## Hazard warning and protection

**3.17**   Are pedestrian and vehicular routes separated and clearly differentiated?

**3.18**   Is blister tactile paving used to indicate an approaching vehicular route?

**3.19**   Is hazard protection provided to any object that projects into a pedestrian route?

- Does this include a tapping rail?

**3.20**   Does hazard protection contrast visually with the surroundings?

General observations:

# Shared spaces 4

## Layout and features

**4.1**  Is the shared space layout logical and easy to interpret?

**4.2**  Are landmark features such as vistas and distinctive buildings used to aid orientation?

**4.3**  Do gateway features adequately indicate the boundaries of the shared space?

**4.4**  Are courtesy crossing points suitably positioned?
- Located at regular intervals?
- Easy to identify?

**4.5**  Are bus stops suitably located?
- Easy to identify?
- Incorporate a raised kerb with gently sloping surfaces?

**4.6**  Is the building line clear of obstructions?

**4.7**  Is street furniture positioned to minimise clutter and to ensure pedestrian routes are unobstructed?

**4.8**  Are comfort zones continuous and do they link with designated crossing points?

**4.9**  Is the notional carriageway clearly differentiated from the comfort zone in kerb-free areas?

**4.10**  Are surface materials suitable?
- Is there a minimal crossfall gradient to access routes?

**4.11**  Do surface materials of vehicular areas generate road noise as a means of alerting pedestrians?

**4.12**   Are there sufficient areas for general circulation
and social interaction?

- Sufficient seating areas?
- Suitable seating with clear space alongside?

**4.13**   Parking spaces for Blue Badge holders, if
appropriate?

**4.14**   Adequate and well-positioned lighting for all
road users?

- Lights integrated into overall street design
and / or combined with other street furniture?
- Positioned to provide an even level of
illumination and to avoid glare and shadows?

**4.15**   Effective means of surface water drainage to all
areas?

**4.16**   Is signage and wayfinding effective and logical?

- Easy to follow?

General observations:

# Street furniture 5

**5.1** Is street furniture positioned at or beyond the edge of pedestrian access routes?

**5.2** Are potential obstructions clearly identified?

**5.3** Is street furniture logically arranged to minimise clutter?

**5.4** Are seats, litter bins, lighting and signs in convenient locations?

**5.5** Do design features such as visual contrast, changes in texture and lighting help to highlight pedestrian routes?

**5.6** Is seating provided at regular intervals and on long or inclined routes?
- Is the seating suitable?
- Clear space alongside?

**5.7** Adequate headroom to pedestrian route?

**5.8** Guarding and cane-detection provisions to areas with less than 2100mm headroom?

**5.9** Bollards at least 1000mm high and visually contrasting with background?
- Chains and ropes linking bollards avoided?

**5.10** Items of street furniture visually contrasting with background?
- Free-standing posts and columns highlighted using visually contrasting bands at the appropriate height?

**5.11** Cycle parking areas located clear of pedestrian routes and adequately highlighted?

- Space for tandems and adapted cycles?
- Protected from the weather?
- Tapping rail provided?

**5.12** Is signage and wayfinding effective and logical?

- Easy to follow?

General observations:

# External ramps 6

**6.1** Ramp accompanied by steps where the rise is greater than 300mm?

**6.2** Ramp accompanied by an alternative means of access where the total rise is greater than 2000mm?

**6.3** Ramp identifiable from approach route or clearly signed?

**6.4** Ramp length and gradient suitable?

- Overall length of ramp and total rise acceptable?
- Wide enough to full length of ramp slope and landings?
- Ramps wider than 2500mm divided into channels?

**6.5** Maximum cross-fall gradient to ramp slope and landings?

**6.6** Top and bottom landings of adequate size and clear of door swings?

- Intermediate landings at regular intervals and of sufficient length?
- Larger landings provided where it is not possible to see from one end of the ramp to another?

**6.7** Edge protection to any open side of ramp or landing?

- Visually contrasting with ramp and landing surface?

**6.8** Surface suitable?

- Adequate slip resistance in all weather conditions?

**6.9** Slope surface visually contrasting with landings?

**6.10** Adequate and even level of illumination to the full length of the ramp?

- Light fittings selected and positioned to avoid glare?

**6.11** Are portable ramps available in existing buildings where no alternative means of access is possible?

- Suitable width?
- Upturned edges?
- Slip-resistant surface?

See also checklist eight Handrails

General observations:

# External steps 7

| | |
|---|---|
| **7.1** | Steps accompanied by a ramp where the rise is greater than 300mm? |
| **7.2** | Single isolated steps avoided? |
| **7.3** | Steps identifiable from approach route or clearly signed? |
| **7.4** | Consistent step dimensions throughout a flight and to consecutive flights? |
| **7.5** | Step risers and goings within acceptable limits? |
| **7.6** | Step profile suitable and unlikely to trip users? |
| **7.7** | Total rise of flight suitable? |
| **7.8** | Linear stair flight with straight steps? <br>• Tapered and curved steps and flights avoided? |
| **7.9** | Unobstructed width adequate? <br>• Steps wider than 2000mm divided into channels? |
| **7.10** | Intermediate landings long enough and clear of door swings? |
| **7.11** | Adequate cross-fall gradient to steps and landings exposed to the weather? |
| **7.12** | Step and landing surface suitable? <br>• Slip-resistant in all weather conditions? |
| **7.13** | Nosings effectively highlight step edges? |
| **7.14** | Step profile suitable? <br>• Chamfered and profiled nosings designed to minimise the risk of tripping? <br>• Open risers avoided? |

**7.15** Tactile corduroy hazard warning surfacing at top and bottom of steps?

- Of correct style and detail?
- Correctly aligned?

**7.16** Surface finish to steps contrast visually with landing surfaces?

**7.17** Adequate and even level of illumination to the full length of the step flight and landings?

- Light fittings selected and positioned to avoid glare?

See also checklist eight Handrails

General observations:

# Handrails 8

## Repeat checklist for external and internal ramps, steps and stairs

**8.1**    Are handrails provided in conjunction with a change in level?

**8.2**    Is the handrail profile easy to grip and comfortable to use?

- Provide forearm support?
- Suitable cross-section dimensions?
- Adequate clearance from support wall or bracket?

**8.3**    Handrails positioned at a suitable height?

- Above ramp slopes and steps?
- Above landing surfaces?

**8.4**    Continuous along ramp slopes, stair flights and intermediate landings?

**8.5**    Extend beyond the top and bottom of the slope or flight?

**8.6**    Open ends of handrails turned to the horizontal position to indicate transition to the landing?

- Handrail ends designed to reduce the risk of clothing being caught?

**8.7**    Handrail supports positioned to enable a person to run their hand along the full length of the rail?

- Supports sufficiently robust?

**8.8**    Additional lower handrail for children and people of short stature?

**8.9** Handrail surface suitable and not cold to the touch?

**8.10** Handrail surface visually contrasting with the background?
  - Non-reflective?

**8.11** Balustrades to ramps and landings sufficiently robust to withstand impact from powered wheelchairs and scooters?

General observations:

# Entrances                                    9

## Identification, signage and approach

**9.1**   Is the principal entrance (or entrances)
          accessible to everyone?

**9.2**   Are alternative accessible entrances available
          for everyone to use?

**9.3**   Entrance easy to find and positioned logically in
          relation to the approach route?

  • Entrance doors clearly distinguishable?

**9.4**   Is the alternative accessible entrance(s) clearly
          signed from the edge of the site and from the
          principal entrance?

  • Incorporating the International Symbol for
    Access?

**9.5**   All entrances clearly signed and visible from
          approach routes?

**9.6**   A level area provided immediately in front of all
          accessible entrances?

**9.7**   Structural supports clearly identified?

  • Positioned away from pedestrian access
    routes?

**9.8**   Weather protection provided?

**9.9**   Clear view in from outside to aid orientation?

**9.10**  Outward-opening doors adequately guarded or
          recessed?

**9.11**  Revolving doors supplemented with an
          adjacent swing door?

  • Swing door clearly visible?

  • Always available?

## Threshold and surfaces

**9.12** Entrance door threshold flush or with minimal upstand and gradual change in level?

- Adjacent floor finishes firmly fixed?

**9.13** Drainage channels adjacent to door thresholds flush with adjacent surfaces?

**9.14** Thresholds to internal doors flush with floor finishes on either side?

- Edges of floor finishes firmly fixed?

**9.15** Entrance matting extends sufficiently into building?

- Suitable, non-compressible material?

- Firmly fixed (loose-laid mats avoided)?

## Entrance lobbies

**9.16** Lobby large enough to allow people to move clear of one door before negotiating the second?

- Arranged for straight through travel?

**9.17** Double swing doors to enable travel in both directions?

**9.18** Lobbies with single-leaf doors large enough?

**9.19** Inner lobby door meets same criteria as entrance door?

**9.20** Lighting designed to provide gradual transition between exterior and interior?

**9.21** Full-height glazing incorporates markings for safety and visibility?

- Minimal reflections?

**9.22** Projections into access route minimised?

- Adequately highlighted or guarded where unavoidable?

General observations:

# Doors – external and internal 　　　**10**

**Repeat checklist for different door types**

## Door dimensions

**10.1** Is the effective clear door width suitable for:

- Entrance doors?
- Inner lobby doors?
- Internal doors?

**10.2** Is sufficient clear manoeuvring space available adjacent to the opening edge of the door?

- If not, is a power-operated door opening system provided?

## Vision panels

**10.3** Vision panels provided to entrance and entrance lobby doors?

**10.4** Vision panels provided to internal corridor doors?

- Doors located on emergency exit routes?
- To side panels of leaf-and-a-half doors?

**10.5** Zone of visibility large enough?

- Suitable configuration?
- Suitable position?

**10.6** Acceptable justification where vision panels are omitted or reduced in size?

## Glazed doors

**10.7** Markings for safety and visibility to glazed doors and side panels?

- Suitable size and height?
- Effective when viewed from both sides?
- Effective in different lighting conditions?

**10.8** Glazed door markings different to adjacent
glazed screen markings?

**10.9** Sides and edges of glass doors adequately
highlighted where adjacent to a glazed screen?

**10.10** Fully glazed doors avoided on corridors?

**10.11** Guarding provided where fully glazed doors
may be held open?

## Door markings

**10.12** Adequate visual contrast to the leading edge of:

- Doors that are held open?
- Outward-opening doors to an internal access
  route?

General observations:

# Doors – access control systems 11

## Entry systems

**11.1** Entry system controls positioned within reach of all users?

- Clearly visible?

**11.2** Clear unobstructed approach?

- On level ground?
- Positioned away from columns and return walls?

**11.3** Entry systems contrast visually with mounting surface?

- Adequately lit?

## Entryphones

**11.4** Entryphone suitable for both audible and visual communication?

Provides audible and visual acknowledgement of call and lock release?

Includes an LED text display to duplicate audible information?

**11.5** Controls simple to use?

- Call buttons easy to identify?
- Tactile symbols?
- Effective visual contrast?

## Security devices

**11.6** Cards or fobs to security devices easy for all to use?

**11.7** Swipe card readers positioned in suitable location?

- Orientated vertically?

## Turnstiles

**11.8**   At least one hinged gate provided where
turnstiles and ticket-control barriers are located?

- Wide enough?
- Suitable for wheelchair access?

General observations:

# Doors – opening and closing systems  **12**

## Door furniture

**12.1**  Door handles to manually operated doors with a latch easy to operate?

- Useable with a single hand without the need to grip and twist?
- Of a suitable size?
- Within reach of all users?

**12.2**  D-type pull handles of a suitable size?

- Within reach of all users?
- Located on the pull side of a door only?

**12.3**  Horizontal grabrails provided to outward-opening doors?

- At a suitable height?

**12.4**  Door handles and grabrails contrast visually with the door?

**12.5**  Hinges appear strong enough and suitable for door size?

**12.6**  Pivot hinges and emergency release bolts provided to inward-opening doors where outward opening may be required in an emergency?

**12.7**  Modified strike plates with a gravity cam provided to doors fitted with mechanical self-closing devices?

- Self-closing force adequate for door to close fully?

**12.8**  Keyways positioned above door handle?

- Or below handle, but with adequate clearance?

**12.9**  Large winged-turns or levers provided to operate snibs and locks?

**12.10** Door bolts easy to reach and operate?

**12.11** Emergency exit devices easy to operate?

- Within reach of all users?

## Door self-closing devices

**12.12** Self-closing device closes door completely?

- But without using excessive closing force?
- Site-adjustable?
- Regularly maintained?

**12.13** Force required to open a door within acceptable limits?

**12.14** Force exerted by self-closing device during closing within acceptable limits?

**12.15** Delayed-action facility available?

**12.16** Backcheck does not reduce the effective clear opening width?

**12.17** Self-closing devices avoided where no mandatory requirements for their use?

## Door hold-open devices

**12.18** Swing-free devices used for inward-opening room doors?

**12.19** Appropriate use of hold-open devices for doors on circulation routes?

- Clearly identifiable manual release button within reach?

**12.20** All devices tested regularly to ensure fail-safe in the event of power failure?

## Power-operated doors

**12.21** Power-operated opening and closing systems used in appropriate locations?

- Clearly identifiable?
- Avoided for doors positioned at the top or bottom of ramps or sloping floors?
- Avoided for swing doors opening across an access route?

**12.22** Clear, direct and level approach to doors?

**12.23** Fully automatic doors provided where access to buildings is freely available?

**12.24** Appropriate use of security devices where controlled access is required?

- Hands-free proximity readers?

**12.25** Speed of door opening and closing suitable for people who move slowly?

- Door fully open as person approaches?

**12.26** Automatic doors include the appropriate signage?

- Indicate direction of opening?

**12.27** Appropriate use of manually activated door controls where fully automatic doors are not suitable?

**12.28** Controls for manually activated doors suitable for all users?

Correctly positioned?

Clearly identifiable?

**12.29** Presence and motion detectors to all power-operated doors?

**12.30** Manual operation possible to all doors in the event of a power failure?

General observations:

# Entrance foyers                                    13

## Layout and orientation

**13.1**   Clear view in from outside to aid orientation?

**13.2**   Routes from entrance doors / lobby logical,
           clearly defined and unobstructed?

**13.3**   Adequate circulation space?

**13.4**   Reception counter suitably positioned?

- Located away from the entrance doors where
  external noise levels are high?

See also checklist 14 Reception desks and
service counters

**13.5**   Clear signage highlighting location of
           reception, WCs, stairs or lift?

- Signs to other parts of the building, where
  relevant?

**13.6**   Signage clear and well designed?

- Incorporates pictograms and symbols?
- Tactile and visual information?

**13.7**   Suitable seating provided?

- Clear space available alongside seating?

## Surface finishes

**13.8**   Suitable floor finishes throughout foyer?

- Firm, smooth and level?
- Slip-resistant?

**13.9**   Flush junctions between different floor
           finishes?

- All edges firmly fixed?

**13.10**  Creative use of floor finishes to highlight
           circulation routes and seating areas?

## Queuing barriers and rails

**13.11** Queuing barriers and rails positioned and spaced to enable easy access for everyone?

**13.12** Adequate clear space between reception / service desk and queuing area?

**13.13** Queuing barriers and rails contrast visually with surroundings?

**13.14** Permanent barriers incorporate a rigid top rail?

- Robust enough for people to lean on?

- Tapping rail?

**13.15** Bases of barrier posts do not present a tripping hazard?

- Or reduce the width of the queuing channel?

General observations:

# Reception desks and service counters   14

## Location and approach

**14.1**   Reception desks / service counters positioned in suitable location?

- Away from potential sources of noise?
- Positioned away from windows where bright sunlight may create difficulties?

**14.2**   Unobstructed and direct access available to both sides of desk / counter?

**14.3**   Sufficient space to manoeuvre on both staff and visitor / customer sides?

**14.4**   Provision on both sides for wheelchair users?

**14.5**   Alternative quiet area or room nearby?

**14.6**   Floor level the same on both staff and visitor / customer side?

**14.7**   Ramped access to raised floor level, if required, on staff side?

## Detail and surfaces

**14.8**   Counter / desk at two heights?

- Suitable for people seated?
- Suitable for people standing?

**14.9**   Knee recess to lower section of counter?

- On staff side?
- Customer / visitor side?

**14.10**   Counter / desk depth suitable?

**14.11**   Counter / desk width adequate?

**14.12**   Edge profile of counter / desk designed to assist picking up papers and coins?

**14.13**   Adequate visual contrast?

**14.14**   Exposed edges and corners well rounded?

## Communication

**14.15** Sliding glass screens / windows able to open fully?

**14.16** Voice amplification system provided to fixed glazed screens?

**14.17** Counter induction loop provided?
- Clearly signed?
- Available for use at all times?

**14.18** Where more than one induction loop is provided, are they adequately spaced to avoid overspill?

**14.19** Artificial lighting suitable?
- Clearly illuminate staff and visitor / customer faces to assist lipreading?

**14.20** Seats available for use at lower level counters / desks?

General observations:

# Seating

# 15

## Provision and layout

**15.1** Seats provided at intervals along long routes or where waiting is likely?

**15.2** Seats set back from pedestrian routes so as not to cause an obstruction?

**15.3** Access to seating direct and unobstructed?

**15.4** Seating positioned on level ground or floor surface?

**15.5** Clear space available alongside fixed seats?

**15.6** Adequate clear space for manoeuvring within rows of seats?
- Space for two wheelchair users to sit along side each other?
- Space for wheelchair user alongside fixed seating?

**15.7** Adequate space to cross aisles in fixed seating?

**15.8** Space for an assistance dog clear of aisles?

## Seating style

**15.9** Seats available at a range of heights?

**15.10** Seats with armrests available?

**15.11** Seats without armrests available to enable wheelchair users to transfer out of their wheelchair?

**15.12** Seats with backs available?

**15.13** Seats within buildings include cushions?

**15.14** Seats available to suit people of larger stature?

**15.15** All seats positioned on a level floor (none on plinths)?

**15.16** Where appropriate, loose seating available to allow for flexible use of space?

**15.17** Perch seats available at a suitable height?

**15.18** Is there adequate visual contrast between seats and background surfaces?

General observations:

# Horizontal circulation 16

## Corridors and passageways

**16.1** Corridor widths adequate for expected use?

**16.2** Circulation routes logical and reasonably direct?

**16.3** Corridor layouts replicated at each floor level, where appropriate?

**16.4** Corridors and passageways unobstructed?

• Wall-mounted fittings recessed?

• Potential obstructions adequately guarded?

**16.5** Corridors allow sufficient space for wheelchair users to turn and pass each other?

• If not, are passing places provided at regular intervals?

• Adequate space at corners and junctions for turning?

**16.6** Are outward-opening doors recessed so as not to obstruct corridor width?

• If not, is location and direction of door opening acceptable?

**16.7** Are corridor doors consistent along a route?

**16.8** Are corridor doors double-swing for ease of use in either direction?

**16.9** Where corridors are narrow, are doors to adjacent areas wider to allow easier access?

**16.10** In sports buildings, do corridor widths take account of the increased width of sports wheelchairs?

## Open-plan areas

**16.11** Are circulation route widths adequate?

- Do they meet the guidelines for corridor widths?

**16.12** Are circulation routes clearly defined?

- Floor finishes and textures used to define routes?

- Artificial lighting used to highlight routes?

**16.13** Furniture and displays kept clear of circulation routes?

- When layouts are altered, are circulation routes maintained?

## Aisles to fixed storage

**16.14** Are storage areas accessible to everyone?

- Clearly identified?

**16.15** Is access direct and unobstructed?

**16.16** Aisle widths adequate?

**16.17** Is side and frontal approach to storage available?

## Changes in level

**16.18** All internal circulation routes level?

- If not, are gradients as shallow as possible?

**16.19** Sloped surfaces clearly differentiated from adjacent level surfaces?

- Level rest area for every 500mm rise where gradient between 1:60 and 1:20?

**16.20** Slopes with gradient greater than 1:20 designed as a ramp?

(See checklist 18)

**16.21** For changes in level greater than 300mm, steps provided in addition to ramp?

**16.22** Where corridors are divided into a sloping and level section, are exposed edges clearly identified?

- Protected by guarding?

## Surface finishes and lighting

**16.23** Effective visual contrast between wall, floor and ceiling surfaces?

- Doors, door frame and wall surfaces?

**16.24** Wall and floor surfaces minimise light reflection?

- And sound reverberation?

**16.25** Bold patterns in flooring avoided?

**16.26** Adequate levels of illumination to circulation routes?

- Light fittings selected and positioned to avoid glare, shadows and silhouettes?

**16.27** Screening provided to windows positioned at the end of corridors?

General observations:

# Surfaces 17

## Floors

**17.1** Floor surfaces firm, level and slip-resistant?

- Suitable for foot and wheeled traffic?

**17.2** Entrance matting effective at removing water and dirt from footwear and wheels?

**17.3** Junctions between floor surfaces correctly detailed and level?

- All edges firmly fixed?

**17.4** Similar slip resistance between adjacent surfaces?

- If not, do surfaces contrast visually?

**17.5** Carpets have shallow dense pile?

**17.6** Shiny and reflective floor surfaces avoided?

**17.7** Floor surfaces with bold patterns avoided?

**17.8** Colours, tones and textures used creatively to help people distinguish between surfaces?

- And highlight potential hazards?

## Walls

**17.9** Wall surfaces plain (not busy or distracting)?

**17.10** Shiny and reflective wall surfaces avoided?

**17.11** Acceptable difference in light reflectance values (LRVs) between wall, floor and ceiling surfaces?

**17.12** Acceptable difference in LRVs for doors, door frames and door handles?

**17.13** Textured wall surfaces used creatively to indicate location of particular facilities?

## Glazed screens and walls

**17.14** Markings for safety and visibility to glazed screens and walls?

- Suitable size and height?
- Effective when viewed from both sides?
- Effective in different lighting conditions?

**17.15** Glazed wall / screen markings different to adjacent glazed door markings?

**17.16** Low light reflectance to glazed screens to reception desks and counters?

**17.17** High-contrast strip to all edges of freestanding glazed screens?

## Ceilings

**17.18** Ceiling surfaces non-reflective?

General observations:

# Internal ramps, steps and stairs   **18**

## Internal ramps

**18.1**    Ramp provided where change in level is less than 300mm?

**18.2**    Ramp accompanied by steps where the rise is greater than 300mm?

**18.3**    Ramp easy to identify or clearly signed?

**18.4**    Ramp length and gradient suitable?

- Overall length of ramp and total rise acceptable?
- Wide enough to full length of ramp slope and landings?
- Ramps wider than 2500mm divided into channels?

**18.5**    Top and bottom landings of adequate size and clear of door swings?

- Intermediate landings at regular intervals and of sufficient length?
- Larger landings provided where it is not possible to see from one end of the ramp to another?

**18.6**    Edge protection to any open side of ramp or landing?

- Visually contrasting with ramp and landing surface?

**18.7**    Suitable slip-resistant surface?

- Slip resistance maintained if ramp at risk of getting wet?

**18.8**    Slope surface visually contrasting with landings?

**18.9**   Adequate and even level of illumination to the full length of the ramp?

  • Light fittings selected and positioned to avoid glare?

**18.10**   Are portable ramps available in existing buildings where no alternative means of access is possible?

  • Suitable width?

  • Upturned edges?

  • Slip-resistant surface?

Also refer to checklist eight Handrails

## Internal steps and stairs

**18.11**   Non-enclosed steps and stairs positioned away from main circulation routes?

  • Deliberate change in direction required to access steps and stairs?

**18.12**   Steps accompanied by a ramp where the rise is greater than 300mm?

**18.13**   Single isolated steps avoided?

**18.14**   Steps identifiable from circulation route or clearly signed?

**18.15**   Consistent step dimensions throughout a flight and to consecutive flights?

**18.16**   Step risers and goings within acceptable limits?

**18.17**   Total rise of flight suitable?

**18.18**   Linear stair flight with straight steps?

  • Tapered and curved steps and flights avoided?

**18.19**   Unobstructed width adequate?

  • Steps wider than 2000mm divided into channels?

**18.20**   Intermediate landings long enough and clear of door swings?

**18.21** Suitable slip-resistant surface?

- Slip resistance maintained if steps at risk of getting wet?

**18.22** Nosings effectively highlight step edges?

Step profile suitable?

- Chamfered and profiled nosings designed to minimise the risk of tripping?
- Open risers avoided?

**18.23** Surface finish to steps contrast visually with landing surfaces?

**18.24** Adequate and even level of illumination to the full length of the step flight and landings?

- Light fittings selected and positioned to avoid glare?

Also refer to checklist eight Handrails

General observations:

# Passenger lifts 19

## Lift provision

**19.1** Passenger lift available in a building of more than one storey?

- Lift serves all floor levels, including basement(s)?

**19.2** Total number of lifts appropriate for size of building and patterns of use?

**19.3** Size(s) of lift(s) meets the needs of all building users?

**19.4** At least one lift available with a minimum lift car size 1400mm deep x 1100mm wide?

**19.5** Lift available with internal lift car size 1400mm deep x 2000mm wide?

**19.6** In sports buildings, lift size able to accommodate sports wheelchairs?

**19.7** Lift door arrangement at each floor level provides convenient access for wheelchair users?

**19.8** Lift easy to identify or clearly visible from building entrance?

**19.9** Access to lift is direct, unobstructed and step-free?

## Lift landing areas

**19.10** Clear landing area in front of lift doors at all floor levels?

- Landing areas separate from circulation routes?

- Lift landings positioned away from stair flight?

**19.11** Lift call buttons clearly visible?

- Contrast visually with mounting plate?

- Mounting plate contrasts visually with surrounding wall?

**19.12** Call button symbols embossed?

- Buttons illuminate when pressed?

**19.13** Call buttons within reach of all users?

**19.14** Visual and audible indication of lift arrival?

- And direction of travel?

**19.15** Lift landing floor and wall surfaces contrast visually with lift doors?

**19.16** Visual and tactile indication of floor level adjacent to lift call buttons?

- Opposite the lift doors?

## Lift door and interior

**19.17** Lift door wide enough?

**19.18** Door remains open long enough to allow slow entry and exit?

**19.19** A light-curtain or photo-eye safety device installed to prevent the door closing if the doorway is obstructed?

**19.20** Control panel(s) in suitable location?

- At suitable height?
- Duplicate controls to side walls of larger lift cars?

**19.21** Extra-large (XL) controls provided for increased accessibility?

**19.22** Control buttons clearly visible?

- Contrast visually with mounting plate and surrounding surface?

**19.23** Control button symbols embossed?

**19.24** Control buttons provide audible and visual feedback when pressed?

**19.25** Audible announcement and visual display within lift car to indicate floor level reached?

**19.26** Handrail available to at least one side wall?

- Appropriate height and size?

**19.27** Emergency communication system available?

- Easy to use?
- Push-button activation?
- Intercom panel (not a handset)?
- Volume control and inductive coupler?
- Additional communication system close to floor level?

**19.28** Alarm buttons provide audible and visual acknowledgement that alarm has been raised?

**19.29** Lift car floor surface has similar level of slip-resistance to lift landings?

**19.30** Lift car floor light in colour?

**19.31** Adequate and even level of illumination within lift car?

- Light fittings selected and positioned to avoid glare and shadows?

**19.32** Mirror provided to rear wall of lift with a lift car 1100mm wide x 1400mm deep?

- Bottom edge of mirror no lower than 900mm?

**19.33** Fold-down seat available in larger lifts?

**19.34** Glazed walls and doors to lifts incorporate markings for safety and visibility?

- Glazed lift floors avoided?

**19.35** Lifts designated for emergency evacuation fitted with an independent power supply?

- Located in a fire-protected shaft?
- Meet additional guidance set out in BS 9999 for evacuation lifts?

General observations:

# Platform lifts 20

**20.1** Platform lift available as an alternative means of access to an adjacent stair or ramp?

**20.2** Location clearly defined by visual and tactile information?

**20.3** Direct and unobstructed access?

**20.4** External platform lifts sufficiently protected from the weather?

**20.5** Designed and available for independent use?

**20.6** Clear instructions for use?

**20.7** Platform adequately guarded or enclosed?

**20.8** Platform dimensions suitable for a wheelchair user and companion?

- Fold-down seat available?

**20.9** Clear landing space available at each floor level?

**20.10** Platform doors and gates: outward opening and wide enough for wheelchair users?

- Visually contrasting with adjacent walls and floor?
- Minimal opening pressure or power-assisted controls?
- Door handles / controls within reach of all users?

**20.11** Landing controls within reach of all users?

- Distinguishable against background?

**20.12** Lift car controls, including emergency call, located easily and within reach of all users?

- Symbols embossed and visually contrasting with face plate?
- Easy to use?

**20.13** Audible and visual indication of platform movement, direction of travel and floor level reached?

**20.14** Two-way emergency voice communication system provided?

- Easy to use?

**20.15** Handrail available to at least one side wall?

- Appropriate height and size?

**20.16** Platform floor level with landing floor at lowest boarding point?

- If not, shallow access ramp to bridge change in level?

## Non-enclosed platform lifts

**20.17** Non-enclosed platform lifts rise no higher than 2000mm?

**20.18** Gates and guarding provided to the upper floor level served by non-enclosed platform lift?

- Adequate height?
- If higher than 1100mm, the gate / door incorporates a vision panel?

**20.19** Fixed guarding to low-rise platform lifts adequate height?

- Incorporate a mid-rail and kick plate?

**20.20** Fixed guarding to platform lifts rising more than 1000mm adequate height?

- Incorporate a kick plate and suitable guarding with solid panels or vertical bars?

## Enclosed platform lifts

**20.21** Platform lift enclosed if vertical travel 2000mm or more?

**20.22** Platform lift enclosed if the lift penetrates a floor?

## Inclined platform stairlifts

**20.23** Exceptional circumstances to justify the continued use of an inclined platform stairlift?

**20.24** Platform size adequate?

**20.25** Clear access route onto and off the platform at top and bottom landing?

**20.26** Controls designed to prevent unauthorised use?

**20.27** Means of communicating with staff available?

- And means of summoning assistance?

**20.28** In buildings with a single stair, is the required width for means of escape maintained between the handrail and stairlift rail?

- Is a clear width of 600mm maintained when the platform is in use?

- Is consultation with the fire officer recommended?

General observations:

# Sanitary facilities 21

## Overall provision

**21.1**  At least one unisex accessible WC provided in each location where toilets available?

- Close to the building entrance / waiting area?

**21.2**  Accessible WC provided in single-sex toilet areas?

**21.3**  Suitable accessible WC available to disabled employees?

- Within a reasonable distance?

**21.4**  Enlarged unisex accessible WC provided where only one toilet in building?

- Includes a corner-arrangement accessible WC?
- And standing-height washbasin?

**21.5**  Cubicle for ambulant disabled people available in single-sex WC areas?

- Adequate room size?
- Outward-opening door with horizontal rail?
- Unobstructed activity space?
- Support rails?

**21.6**  Changing Places toilet provided in larger public buildings?

(See also checklist items under Changing Places toilets)

**21.7**  Accessible urinal in male WC area?

- Support rails?

**21.8**  Lower-height washbasin provided in a suite of washbasins?

**21.9**  Location of WC clearly signed?

## Doors and locks

**21.10** Doors to WC cubicles and accessible WCs outward opening?

- Horizontal rail to assist door closing?
- Mechanical self-closing devices not used?

**21.11** Doors capable of being opened in an emergency?

**21.12** Facility indicator easy to use?

- Includes text and colour to indicate when in use?

**21.13** Accessible WCs highlighted with International Symbol for Access?

## Sanitaryware and accessories

**21.14** Slip-resistant floors throughout?

- Slip-resistance maintained when wet?

**21.15** Shiny floor and wall surfaces avoided?

**21.16** Surfaces and fixtures provide effective visual contrast?

**21.17** Toilet seat height suitable?

**21.18** Wall-mounted handrails suitable diameter?

- Adequate clearance from wall?
- Easy to grip?

**21.19** Drop-down support rails provided?

- Firmly held when not in use?
- Easy to release when required?
- Sufficiently strong and securely fixed?

**21.20** Clothes hooks provided at two heights?

- Suitably positioned?

**21.21** Toilet paper and paper towel dispensers suitable?

- Designed for single-hand operation?

**21.22** Privacy screens to urinals?

## Heating, lighting and water supply

**21.23** Washbasin taps easy to operate?

**21.24** Water temperature regulated?

**21.25** Water supply and waste pipes boxed in?

- Positioned away from manoeuvring space?

**21.26** Heat emitters limited to a safe temperature?

- Positioned away from manoeuvring space?

**21.27** Light switch or pull cord clearly visible?

- Visually contrasting?

**21.28** Emergency lighting available?

## Alarms

**21.29** Emergency assistance alarm provided in appropriate facilities?

- Positioned correctly?
- Alarms linked to a staffed area?
- Incorporate visual and audible indicators?

**21.30** Alarm pull cords suitable?

**21.31** Fire alarms audible and visible within all WC areas?

## Unisex accessible corner WC

**21.32** Are room dimensions adequate?

**21.33** If more than one accessible WC is provided, are the layouts handed?

- Is the handing indicated on signage?

**21.34** Overall provision of sanitaryware and accessories suitable?

- Correctly positioned?

**21.35** Manoeuvring area free from obstruction?

**21.36** Toilet flush handle within reach and easy to operate?

**21.37** Hand washing and drying facilities within easy reach of someone seated on WC?

- Taps easy to operate?
- Temperature controlled?

## Accessible baby-changing facilities

**21.38** Accessible baby-changing facilities provided?

- Located separately from single-sex WC areas?

**21.39** Are room dimensions adequate?

**21.40** Baby-changing bench provided?

- Suitable height or height adjustable?

**21.41** Washbasin provided at suitable height?

**21.42** Adequate disposal bins?

- Positioned so as not to cause obstruction?

**21.43** Nappy vending machine within reach?

## Prayer washing facilities

**21.44** Are male and female prayer washing facilities segregated?

**21.45** Accessible facilities provided in both male and female areas?

- Step-free floor surface to at least one washing position?
- Unobstructed access?
- Adequate manoeuvring space?
- Support rails?

**21.46** Non-slip floor surface?

- Slip-resistance maintained when wet?

**21.47** Seats provided at different heights or height adjustable?

**21.48** Coat hooks and hand dryers at a range of heights?

**21.49** Footwear storage at a range of heights?

## Changing Places toilets

**21.50** Is a Changing Places (CP) toilet provided?

**21.51** CP toilet clearly signed?

- Signage incorporates the CP symbol?

**21.52** Convenient unobstructed approach route?

**21.53** CP toilet located close to customer service staff?

**21.54** Signage indicating location of nearest unisex accessible toilet and baby-changing facility clearly displayed?

## Room layout and equipment

**21.55** Room size at least 3000mm x 4000mm?

- Ceiling height adequate?

**21.56** Door arrangement suitable?

- Wide enough?
- Handles and grab rails suitable?

**21.57** Overall provision of sanitaryware, equipment and accessories suitable?

- Positioned to enable easy transfer?
- Sufficient space for assistant(s)?

**21.58** Clear manoeuvring space available?

## WC fixtures

**21.59** Peninsular toilet arrangement?

**21.60** Toilet incorporates a backrest and suitable seat?

- Robust installation?

**21.61** Shelf for colostomy bags provided close to WC and at approriate height?

**21.62** Support rails provided?

- Fold-down rails suitable?

**21.63** Height-adjustable washbasin provided?

- Clear knee space below bowl?

- Taps easy to use?

- Water temperature limited to a safe level?

**21.64** Hand drying facilities close to washbasin?

**21.65** Privacy screen available?

## Hoist equipment

**21.66** Hoist equipment available?

- Full-room cover?

- Safe working load at least 200kg?

**21.67** Range of sling types compatible with hoist?

- Information about sling compatibility available to users in advance of a visit?

**21.68** Handset controls easy to use?

- Auxiliary controls located on motor unit?

- Emergency stopping and lowering facility?

- Return-to-charge feature in convenient location?

**21.69** Clear instructions for use?

## Changing bench

**21.70** Height-adjustable changing bench available?

- Height-adjustment range suitable?

- Adequate size?

**21.71** Either mains powered or battery powered?

**21.72** Safe working load at least 200kg?

**21.73** Surface suitable for changing and showering?

**21.74** Adjustable backrest?

**21.75** Wide paper roll dispenser available?

## Shower facilities

**21.76** Shower available adjacent to changing bench?

**21.77** Shower seat available?

**21.78** Wet room floor with suitable drainage?

**21.79** Shower controls mounted within reach of users?

- Hose long enough to reach the full length of the changing bench?
- Water temperature adjustable but limited to a safe level?

## Alarms

**21.80** Assistance alarm provided?

- Pull cords or wands in two locations?
- Alarms linked to a staffed area?
- Incorporate visual and audible indicators?

**21.81** Alarm pull cords suitable?

**21.82** Fire alarm audible and visible within room?

## Surfaces

**21.83** Suitable slip-resistant floor surface?

**21.84** Effective visual contrast between surfaces and fixtures?

## Accessories

**21.85** Separate disposal bins provided for general waste and personal care items?

- Positioned so as not to obstruct manoeuvring space?

**21.86** Clothes hooks provided at two heights?

**21.87** Long mirror provided?

**21.88** Is the room clear and well ventilated?

General observations:

# Wayfinding, information and signs  **22**

## Layout, features and landmarks

**22.1**  Overall layout of building reasonably clear and logical?

**22.2**  Entrance and exit routes obvious?

**22.3**  Landmark features used to aid navigation?

**22.4**  Key facilities located in similar position on each floor level?

**22.5**  Creative use of colour coding to signal location of key facilities?

**22.6**  Visual contrast used effectively to define features and spaces?

**22.7**  Where information is conveyed using textured surfaces, is a key available at a central point?
- Easy to understand?

## Provision and location of signs

**22.8**  Logical and consistent use of signs?
- Suitable for all building users?

**22.9**  Information and directional signs positioned in key locations?

**22.10**  Accessible routes and accessible exits clearly highlighted?

**22.11**  Signage design, layout and positioning consistent?

**22.12**  Directional signage provided to enable people to return to their starting point?
- To locate a particular exit?

## Visual signs

**22.13** Effective visual contrast between letters, symbols, pictograms and signboard?

- Between signboard and mounting surface?
- Adequate difference in LRV?

**22.14** Signs short, simple and easy to understand?

**22.15** Sans serif typeface?

**22.16** Text written with initial capital letter and then lower case?

- Words in all capital letters avoided?

**22.17** Signs positioned so as not to cause an obstruction?

**22.18** Directional signs mounted at high level in busy or crowded areas?

**22.19** Room name signs positioned on wall adjacent to leading edge of door?

- WC door signs positioned on door?

**22.20** Wall-mounted signs at suitable height?

- Signs duplicated at two heights where appropriate?

**22.21** Text height suitable for viewing distance?

**22.22** Signs well lit?

**22.23** Sign surface is matt and / or non-reflective?

## Symbols and pictograms

**22.24** Symbols and pictograms used as well as text where possible?

**22.25** Symbols and pictograms large enough?

**22.26** Accessible facilities identified using appropriate symbol?

**22.27** Standard public information symbols used appropriately?

## Tactile signs

**22.28** Tactile information provided in addition to visual information?

**22.29** Tactile signs positioned within reach?

**22.30** Embossed text easy to read by touch?

## Braille

**22.31** Braille information provided in addition to embossed text and symbols?

**22.32** Appropriate use of Grade one and Grade two Braille?

**22.33** Braille positioned within reach?

- Identified using a Braille locator?
- Supplemented with an embossed arrow where necessary?

**22.34** Frames and raised borders avoided for Braille signs?

## Tactile maps and models

**22.35** Portable tactile maps available?

**22.36** Three-dimensional models available?

**22.37** Maps and models clear and uncluttered?

- Include a north point?
- Bar scale?
- Key to symbols and textures?
- Braille and audible instruction available?

## Audible signs and electronic navigation systems

**22.38** Talking signs provided in suitable environments?

- Clearly advertised?
- Informative?

**22.39** Personal receivers / headsets available to borrow, where applicable?

General observations:

# Communication systems and acoustics **23**

## Telephones for public use

**23.1** Are telephones located where there is minimal background noise?

**23.2** At least one telephone accessible to wheelchair users?

- Clear space available for frontal and side approach?
- Keypads and other controls positioned at a suitable height?

**23.3** Telephones available at a height to suit standing users?

- Adjacent seat provided?
- Support rails adjacent to seating?

**23.4** Text and email payphones available in addition to standard telephones?

**23.5** Keypads well lit and visually contrasting?

**23.6** Adjacent shelf available next to all public telephones?

**23.7** Inductive coupler and volume control available to all public telephones?

**23.8** Telephone booth or room adequate size?

**23.9** Clearly written instructions available?

**23.10** Effective visual contrast between equipment and surfaces?

**23.11** Signs to accessible telephones incorporate the International Symbol for Access?

## Public address systems

**23.12** Are spoken announcements clearly audible?

- Speakers located at intervals throughout building?

**23.13** Are announcements consistent with visual
information?

**23.14** Public address systems linked to induction
loops?

## Hearing enhancement systems

**23.15** Hearing enhancement systems available in
suitable locations?

**23.16** Type of system suitable for location and
expected use?

**23.17** More than one type of system available where
appropriate?

**23.18** All hearing enhancement systems signed with
correct symbol?

**23.19** All systems regularly tested?

- User trials?
- Equipment trials?

**23.20** Input sockets for multimedia presentations
positioned in accessible locations?

**23.21** Microphone faults detectable using monitoring
equipment?

**23.22** Induction loops located where overspill will not
compromise confidentiality?

**23.23** Induction loops positioned away from sources
of potential magnetic interference?

- Away from significant amounts of metal
within the building structure?

**23.24** Infrared systems provided in suitable locations?

- Sufficient number of headsets and receivers
available?
- Procedures in place to store, issue, return
and clean headsets and receivers?

**23.25** Radio systems used in suitable locations?

- Located away from sources of potential magnetic interference?
- Sufficient number of headsets and receivers available?
- Procedures in place to store, issue, return and clean headsets and receivers?

**23.26** Soundfield systems installed in suitable locations?

- Linked to other hearing enhancement systems to enable use of single microphone?

## Acoustics

**23.27** Areas such as reception and service desks located away from noise sources?

**23.28** Traffic noise minimised by suitable placement of windows?

**23.29** Building structure adequately insulated against the passage of sound?

**23.30** Quiet and noisy areas of the building separated by a buffer zone?

**23.31** Balance of hard and soft surfaces within rooms and spaces?

**23.32** Mechanical equipment positioned where the noise they generate will not cause difficulties?

- Adequately maintained to minimise noise in use?

**23.33** Mains electrical cabling positioned away from public areas?

General observations:

# Switches and controls 24

**24.1** Controls, switches and mounting plates contrast visually with mounting surface?

**24.2** Instructions for equipment use clearly displayed?

- Positioned adjacent to corresponding controls?
- Able to be read at close range?
- Tactile as well as visual?

**24.3** Electrical power sockets all switched?

- **ON** and **OFF** positions clearly identifiable?

**24.4** Large rocker switches for lights available?

**24.5** Panels with multiple switches arranged with adequate space between each switch?

- All switches clearly labelled?

**24.6** Electrical mains and circuit isolator switches clearly labelled?

- **ON** and **OFF** positions easy to identify?

**24.7** Red and green switch indicators supplemented with text and / or graphics?

**24.8** All switches and controls operable with one hand?

**24.9** Switches and controls positioned in consistent locations throughout building?

- At a suitable height?
- With adequate clearance from return walls?

General observations:

# Lighting                                    **25**

**25.1**    Lighting designed to meet a wide range of users' needs?

**25.2**    Level of lighting sufficient for intended use?
- PIR-activated booster lighting available?

**25.3**    Can building users control and adjust artificial lighting?
- Natural lighting?

**25.4**    Stairs, other changes in level and potential hazards well lit?

**25.5**    Lighting at reception desks and speaker rostrums positioned to illuminate a person's face?
- Lighting available to illuminate sign language interpreters?

**25.6**    Lights positioned where they do not cause glare, reflection, confusing shadows or pools of light and dark?

**25.7**    Windows, blinds and lamps all kept clean?

**25.8**    Fluorescent lighting installed only where it is unlikely to cause inconvenience to people with hearing impairments?
- Artificial lighting compatible with other electronic and radio frequency installations?

**25.9**    Lighting does not undermine effectiveness of visual contrast in colour schemes?

General observations:

# Building management     **26**

Are the following issues addressed by building management and checked on a regular basis:

## External areas

## Car parking

**26.1**    Information available to visitors in advance of a visit?

**26.2**    Car parking: designated spaces not used by non-disabled drivers?

- Kept clear of obstructions?

**26.3**    Parking bays allocated to disabled staff clearly marked to discourage use by others?

**26.4**    Entry and exit barriers incorporate means of communication with staff?

- Staff able to provide assistance?

## Pedestrian routes

**26.5**    External routes, including steps and ramps, kept clean, unobstructed and free of surface water, algae growth, snow and ice?

**26.6**    Surface materials maintained in good condition?

- Potential trip hazards repaired?

**26.7**    Bicycles not parked or chained where they will obstruct steps, ramps or access routes?

**26.8**    Vegetation and planting kept trimmed to avoid:

- Overhanging access routes?
- Obscuring signage and the spread of light?

**26.9**    Effective enforcement in shared space areas:

- Traffic speed limits?
- Delivery access?
- Parking restrictions?

**26.10** External lights in good working order?

- Bulbs replaced promptly?

## Buildings

## Entrances

**26.11** Where necessary, are portable ramps available?

- Removed promptly after use?

**26.12** Are side-hung doors adjacent to revolving doors unlocked?

- Freely available whenever the building is open?

**26.13** Access control systems tested regularly?

**26.14** Door opening and closing systems tested regularly?

**26.15** Timing and speed of power-operated devices reviewed and adjusted regularly?

**26.16** Procedures in place to ensure staff are always available to respond to entryphone systems?

- Available to provide assistance if required?

## Doors

**26.17** Door ironmongery regularly maintained and adjusted if necessary?

**26.18** Door self-closing devices monitored and adjusted when necessary?

## Circulation routes

**26.19** Circulation routes kept clear of obstructions, including deliveries?

**26.20** Clear space maintained in front of lift doors, signage, waste bins and water coolers, and so on?

**26.21** Space maintained between moveable seats and tables?

## Lifts

**26.22** Statutory tests and servicing of lifts and platform lifts undertaken regularly?

- Arranged at times to minimise inconvenience to building users?

**26.23** Procedures in place to provide alternative means of access if lifts or platform lifts are out of action?

- Are arrangements clearly communicated?

**26.24** Emergency call and communication systems in lifts and platform lifts tested regularly?

- Is the system linked to a source of assistance?

**26.25** Alignment of lift car floor with landing floors checked regularly?

## Surfaces

**26.26** Edges of floor coverings firmly fixed?

- Door threshold strips?

**26.27** Worn floor finishes replaced before they present a trip hazard or fail to provide adequate slip resistance?

**26.28** Floor surfaces regularly cleaned?

- But not left shiny or slippery?

**26.29** Effective visual contrast maintained or enhanced when areas redecorated?

## Sanitary facilities

**26.30** If accessible WCs or Changing Places (CP) toilets are kept locked, is a key available to lend close by?

- Is the availability of the key clearly indicated?
- Do staff know where the key is located?

**26.31** Is information available to visitors in advance if a RADAR National Key Scheme key is required?

**26.32** Are all components of the toilet assistance alarms regularly checked:

- Pull cords?
- Reset button?
- Responder unit(s)?

**26.33** Are assistance alarm pull cords fully extended and available at all times?

**26.34** Are procedures in place for responding to assistance alarms?

- Are staff trained to provide appropriate assistance?
- Is there always someone available to respond?

**26.35** In CP toilets, are instructions for using equipment clearly displayed?

**26.36** Is information available regarding hoist connectors and compatible slings?

- In advance of a visit?

**26.37** Is mechanical equipment checked and serviced regularly?

**26.38** Are fastenings to toilet seats, fixed and drop-down rails checked regularly?

**26.39** Are all sanitary facilities cleaned and restocked daily (or more often if required)?

**26.40** Are waste bins and disposal units positioned where they will not obstruct access and transfer space?

## Building services

## Maintenance and tests

**26.41** Statutory tests, inspections and servicing arranged for lifts, platform lifts, hoists and other equipment?

- Arranged at times to minimise inconvenience to building users?

**26.42** Procedures in place to ensure light bulbs are replaced promptly?

## Cleaning

**26.43** Mechanical ventilation, air conditioning and heating systems regularly cleaned and maintained?

**26.44** Windows and glazed screens and doors cleaned regularly?

**26.45** Blinds and solar control devices maintained, cleaned and fully functioning?

## Communications

## Information

**26.46** Venue and visitor information available in a range of formats?

**26.47** Pre-visit information available about accessible facilities such as:

- Availability of parking?
- Whether a RADAR National Key Scheme key is required for accessible toilets or CP toilets?
- Equipment provided in CP facility and type of sling connectors?
- Presence of strobe lighting?

**26.48** Audio description available where information is lengthy or complex?

## Hearing enhancement systems

**26.49** Is availability of system clearly advertised?

**26.50** Are staff trained in using the equipment?

**26.51** Are hearing enhancement systems and public address systems regularly tested?

- Equipment tests?
- User trials?

**26.52** Is there an adequate system for lending, retrieving, testing and cleaning headsets?

## Signage

**26.53**  Do new signs integrate with an existing signage system?

**26.54**  Are signs replaced correctly if removed during redecoration?

**26.55**  Are redundant and temporary signs removed when no longer required?

**26.56**  Are maps and models updated when required?

## Means of escape

## Policy and procedures

**26.57**  Are checks made to ensure all internal and external exit routes are clear and unobstructed at all times?

- And that final exit doors are operational and available for use?

**26.58**  Are checks made to ensure access for fire-fighting vehicles is available at all times?

**26.59**  Is the fire alarm system checked regularly?

- Are all audible sounders and visible beacons checked regularly to ensure operational?

**26.60**  Are evacuation tests arranged at regular intervals?

- Are all staff familiar with procedures and duties?

**26.61**  Do building managers liaise regularly with disabled staff and frequent disabled visitors to agree and review individual Personal Emergency Egress Plans?

General observations:

# Information

# 27

**27.1** Is information available in a range of formats, including:

- Clear print?
- Large print?
- Braille?
- Telephone services?
- Audio?
- Digital (for example, disk, CD ROM, DVD or file attachment)?

**27.2** Is the information readily available?

## Clear print

**27.3** Does printed material follow clear print guidelines, including:

- A suitable font style and size?
- Effective contrast between text and back ground?
- A suitable line length and spacing?
- A suitable word spacing and paragraph alignment?
- An avoidance of decorative text, text written at an angle or in curved lines?

**27.4** Are the design and layout simple and uncluttered?

**27.5** Are headings, photos, illustrations and text clearly differentiated?

**27.6** Are photos and illustrations suitably sized?

## Large print

**27.7** Do large print documents follow best practice guidelines, including:

- A suitable font style and size?
- Effective contrast between text and background?

**27.8** Can documents be readily produced in a font size to meet individual customer need?

**27.9** Are large print documents as close as possible in format to the standard print version?

## Braille

**27.10** Is Braille information professionally produced to RNIB guidelines?

**27.11** If any information is not available in Braille, such as a complex and frequently updated catalogue, is an alternative available, for example a telephone information service?

## Telephone services

**27.12** Are contact telephone and textphone numbers clearly advertised and staffed?

**27.13** Are textphone operators trained in the use of the equipment?

**27.14** Are telephone operators familiar with the Text Relay service?

## Audio tape

**27.15** Do audio tapes follow best practice guidelines, including:
- Speaker's voice clearly audible?
- Structure and location of information clearly communicated?
- Effective indexing of sections to enable easy navigation of tape?
- Recording quality good?

## Digital

**27.16** Can information be readily transmitted on disk, CD ROM, DVD or via the internet (using email or downloaded from a website)?

**27.17** Is the document designed in a clear, simple manner?

**27.18** Is the information available (or able to be saved) as a text-only file?

**27.19** Can digital information be tailored to suit individual customer requirements, for example by saving information as a particular file type?

See also checklist 28 Websites

General observations:

# Websites                                    **28**

**28.1**  Has the website been designed in accordance
with best practice guidelines, including:

- Is the website logically structured and easy to
navigate?

- Is language simple and clear?

- Is the font sans serif and commonly available
on most computers?

- Is there effective tonal contrast between text,
graphics and background?

- Is there a text alternative to audio and image
files?

- Are unnecessary moving graphics avoided?

- Are video sequences captioned, or is a link
provided to a transcript of the audio and
video content?

**28.2**  Does the design of the website offer the
flexibility for individual users to adjust text and
colour settings using their own browser?

**28.3**  Is the web designer familiar with international
guidelines on web accessibility?

**28.4**  Does website have WAI or W3C accreditation?

General observations:

# Communication services    **29**

**29.1**    Are staff aware of or given training in the diversity of communication needs?

**29.2**    Are any staff trained and / or qualified to provide communication services?

**29.3**    Is there a procedure for arranging communication services, when required, including:

- British Sign Language (BSL) / English interpreters?
- Communication support workers?
- Deafblind interpreters and communicator guides?
- Lipspeakers?
- Note-takers?
- Electronic note-takers?
- Speech-to-text reporters?

**29.4**    Are communication services offered as an integral part of a programme of events, for example signed, audio described and captioned performances in a theatre?

General observations:

# Appendices

## Organisations

### British Standards Institution (BSI)
Tel: 020 8996 9001
Email: cservices@bsigroup.com
Website: www.bsigroup.com

### Centre for Accessible Environments
Telephone: 020 7822 8232
Email: info@cae.org.uk
Website: www.cae.org.uk

### Changing Places Consortium
For enquiries in England, Wales and Northern Ireland:
Telephone: 020 7696 6019
Email: ChangingPlaces@mencap.org.uk

For enquiries in Scotland:
Telephone: 01382 385 154
Email: PamisChangingPlaces@dundee.ac.uk

Website: www.changing-places.org

### Equality and Human Rights Commission (EHRC)
Helplines:

### England
Telephone: 0845 604 6610
Textphone: 0845 604 6620
Email: englandhelpline@equalityhumanrights.com

### Scotland
Telephone: 0845 604 5510
Textphone: 0845 604 5520
Email: scotlandhelpline@equalityhumanrights.com

### Wales
Telephone: 0845 604 8810
Textphone: 0845 604 8820
Email: waleshelpline@equalityhumanrights.com

Website: www.equalityhumanrights.com

**Equality Commission for Northern Ireland**
Telephone: 028 90 500 600
Textphone: 028 90 500 589
Email: information@equalityni.org
Website: www.equalityni.org

**Business Disability Forum (formerly Employers' Forum on Disability)**
Telephone: 020 7403 3020
Textphone: 020 7403 0040
Email: enquiries@businessdisabilityforum.org.uk
Website: www.businessdisabilityforum.org.uk

**National Register of Access Consultants**
Telephone: 020 7822 8282
Email: info@nrac.org.uk
Website: www.nrac.org.uk

**Northern Ireland Executive**
Telephone: 028 9052 8400
Website: www.northernireland.gov.uk

**Royal Institute of British Architects (RIBA)**
Telephone: 020 7580 5533
Email: info@riba.org
Website: www.architecture.com

**Royal National Institute of Blind People (RNIB)**
Helpline telephone: 0303 123 9999
Email: helpline@rnib.org.uk
Website: www.rnib.org.uk

**Action on Hearing Loss (formerly Royal National Institute for Deaf People)**
Telephone: 0808 808 0123
Textphone: 0808 808 9000
Email: informationline@hearingloss.org.uk
Website: www.actiononhearingloss.org.uk

**Scottish Government**
Telephone: 08457 741 741 or 0131 556 8400
Minicom: 0131 244 1829
Email: ceu@scotland.gsi.gov.uk
Website: www.scotland.gov.uk

**TSO Publications (The Stationery Office)**
Telephone: 0870 600 5522
Email: customer.services@tso.co.uk
Website: www.tsoshop.co.uk

**TSO Ireland**
Telephone: 02890 238451
Email: enquiries@tsoireland.com

**TSO Scotland**
Telephone: 0131 659 7020
Email: enquiries@tsoscotland.com

**Welsh Government**
Telephone: 0300 060 3300 or 0845 010 3300
Email: wag-en@mailuk.custhelp.com
Website: www.wales.gov.uk

## Publications

### Legislation, standards and codes of practice

Building Regulations 2010
Approved Document B: Volume One - dwellinghouses and Volume Two - Buildings other than dwellinghouses (2006 edition incorporating 2010 and 2013 amendments)
*Department for Communities and Local Government*
*NBS, 2013*

Building Regulations 2010
Approved Document K: Protection from falling, collision and impact (2013 edition)
*Department for Communities and Local Government*
*NBS, 2013*

Building Regulations 2010
Approved Document M: Access to and use of buildings (2004 edition incorporating 2010 and 2013 amendments)
*Department for Communities and Local Government*
*NBS, 2013*

Building Regulations (Northern Ireland) 2000
Technical booklet R: Access to and use of buildings 2006
*Department of Finance and Personnel (Northern Ireland)*
*The Stationery Office, 2006*

Building (Scotland) Regulations 2004
2011 Technical Handbooks: Domestic buildings and Non-domestic buildings
*Scottish Executive*
*The Stationery Office, 2011*

Equality Act 2010
*The Stationery Office, 2010*

BS EN 81-1:1998 + A3:2009 Safety rules for the construction and installation of lifts.
*Electric lifts.*
*The British Standards Institution, 1998 (amended 2010)*

BS EN 81-2:1998 + A3:2009 Safety rules for the construction and installation of lifts.
*Hydraulic lifts.*
*The British Standards Institution, 1998 (amended 2010)*

BS EN 81-28:2003 Safety rules for the construction and installation of lifts. Remote alarm on passenger and goods passenger lifts.
*The British Standards Institution, 2003*

BS EN 81-41:2010 Safety rules for the construction and installation of lifts. Special lifts for the transport of persons and goods. Vertical lifting platforms intended for use by persons with impaired mobility.
*The British Standards Institution, 2011*

BS EN 81-70:2003 Safety rules for the construction and installation of lifts. Particular applications for passenger and goods passenger lifts. Accessibility to lifts for persons including persons with disability.
*The British Standards Institution, 2003*

BS 5655-6:2011 Lifts and service lifts. Code of practice for the selection, installation and location of new lifts.
*The British Standards Institution, 2011*

BS 6440:2011 Powered vertical lifting platforms having non-enclosed or partially enclosed liftways intended for use by persons with impaired mobility. Specification.
*The British Standards Institution, 2011*

BS 8300:2009+A1:2010 Design of buildings and their approaches to meet the needs of disabled people - Code of practice
*The British Standards Institution, 2009*

BS 9991:2011 Fire safety in the design, management and use of residential buildings - Code of practice
*The British Standards Institution, 2009*

BS 9999:2008 Code of practice for fire safety in the design, management and use of buildings
*The British Standards Institution, 2008*

National Planning Policy Framework
*Department for Communities and Local Government, 2012*

Statutory Code of Practice: Services, public functions and associations
*The Stationery Office, 2011*
Statutory Code of Practice: Employment
*The Stationery Office, 2011*

What equality law means for you as an education provider – schools
*Equality and Human Rights Commission, 2010*

What equality law means for you as an education provider – further and higher education
*Equality and Human Rights Commission, 2011*

**Other publications**

Accessible Sports Facilities: Design guidance note
*Sport England, 2010*

Accessible Train Station Design for Disabled People: A Code of Practice
*Department for Transport and Transport Scotland, 2011*

Building Bulletin 102 - Children with special educational needs (SEN) and disabilities
*Department for Education, 2012*

Building Sight
*by Peter Barker, Jon Barrick, Rod Wilson*
*HMSO in association with the Royal National Institute of the Blind RNIB, 1995*

Changing Places: A practical guide
*MENCAP and Changing Places Consortium, 2013*

Design and access statements: How to write, read and use them
*Commission for Architecture and the Built Environment, 2006*

Designing for Accessibility
*CAE / RIBA Publishing, 2012*

Easy Access to Historic Buildings
*English Heritage, 2012*

Easy Access to Historic Landscapes
*English Heritage, 2013*

Fire safety risk assessment: Means of escape for disabled people
*Department for Communities and Local Government, 2007*

Good Loo Design Guide
*CAE / RIBA Publishing, 2004*

Guidance on the use of tactile paving surfaces
*Department for Transport, 2005 (updated 2007)*

Health Building Note 00-02: Sanitary spaces
*Department for Health, 2013*

Manual for Streets
*Published for the Department for Transport by Thomas Telford Publishing, 2007*

Sign Design Guide
*by Peter Parker and June Fraser*
*JMU Access Partnership and the Sign Design Society, 2000*
SLL Code for Lighting (Society of Light and Lighting)
*Chartered Institute of Building Services Engineers, 2012*

Specifiers' Handbooks for Inclusive Design:
Architectural Ironmongery
Automatic Door Systems
Internal Floor Finishes
Glass in Buildings
Platform Lifts
*CAE / RIBA Publishing, 2005 and 2006*

Stairs, ramps and escalators: Inclusive design guidance
*CAE / RIBA Publishing, 2010*

The principles of inclusive design. (They include you.)
*Commission for Architecture and the Built Environment, 2006*

Wayfinding: effective wayfinding and signing systems – guidance for healthcare facilities
*The Stationery Office, 2005*

# Index